# Introduction to the New Financial World

## Demystifying Crypto, Defi, Blockchain, and the Global Shift in Finance

Zakir Sadiki

Southern Scribe Press

First Edition - 2025

ISBN: 9798950412028



Visit https://www.newfinancialworld.com to learn more about blockchain education, consulting, and upcoming publications.



For permission requests or inquiries, contact:

Email: info@newfinancialworld.com

Website: https://www.newfinancialworld.com

Publisher: Southern Scribe Press, info@southernscribepress.com

Disclaimer

This book is for educational purposes only and does not constitute financial, investment, tax, or legal advice. The author is not a licensed financial advisor. Cryptocurrency and digital asset markets are highly volatile and carry risk. Readers should perform their own due diligence and consult with a qualified professional before making financial decisions.

Trademarks: Product names, company names, and logos mentioned herein remain the property of their respective owners and are used strictly for identification or educational purposes.

External sources: Any excerpts or quotations from other works are used under fair use for commentary, criticism, or educational illustration and are cited in the Works Cited section.

# Contents

# Acknowledgments

This book would not have been possible without the guidance and expertise of several incredible individuals.

I would like to sincerely thank:

- twitter.com/paulbarron
- twitter.com/DPGmaximus
- twitter.com/mrjakegordon
- twitter.com/Parker_Ray
- twitter.com/APEXCONSULTNFA
- twitter.com/SMQKEDQG
- twitter.com/Chrisharris85

To all of you, and to anyone who shared wisdom, encouragement, or time along this journey - thank you. Your generosity and knowledge have made this book possible.

If you are looking for reputable sources in your crypto journey, I recommend these YouTube channels:

- www.youtube.com/@JakeGordonCrypto
- www.youtube.com/@PaulBarronNetwork
- www.youtube.com/@Parker_Ray
- www.youtube.com/@maximuscrypto2690
- www.youtube.com/@c-zargetscrypto1677
- www.youtube.com/@TheHouseOfCrypto
- www.youtube.com/@ApexCryptoInsights
- www.youtube.com/@MickleXRP
- www.youtube.com/@NoBsCryptoOfficial
- www.youtube.com/@EvanAldo
- www.youtube.com/@blackrue

These channels have been invaluable in helping me learn and understand the rapidly evolving crypto space.

# Introduction to the New Financial World

## The 5th Industrial Revolution

For most of modern history, money moved slowly.

Banks opened in the morning and closed in the evening. Payments took days to settle. International transfers passed through layers of institutions before reaching their destination. The system worked but it was built for a different era.

Today, information moves instantly. A message can travel across the world in seconds. Businesses operate online, and billions of people are connected at all times.

Yet much of the financial system still runs on infrastructure designed decades ago.

That mismatch is starting to matter.

Something is changing.

For many people, it still feels distant. But throughout history, when financial infrastructure shifts, it reshapes how people save, invest, and build wealth.

We may be entering one of those moments now.

To understand why, and what comes next. We need to start with a simple question:

**What is Cryptocurrency?**

Over the past fifteen years, a new type of financial network has quietly emerged-one that operates twenty-four hours a day, seven days a week. On these networks, value can move globally in seconds.

At the center of this shift is something many people have heard of, but few fully understand: cryptocurrency.

Cryptocurrency is digital money secured by cryptography, a method that protects information by transforming it so that only those with the correct key can access it. It runs on decentralized networks using blockchain technology.

Blockchain is a type of database where transactions are grouped into blocks and linked together in a chain, making it challenging to alter records. A distributed ledger, which is a shared record of transactions that multiple computers (called nodes) maintain and agree upon, tracks these actions.

Unlike government-issued money, cryptocurrencies operate without central control, meaning no single organization or country manages or can easily interfere with them. This helps resist interference or manipulation from intermediaries.

Put simply, cryptocurrency is like 'email for money'. Email lets us talk globally without the post office; crypto allows instant, secure payments without banks or government approval.

Cryptocurrencies have limits and face criticism. Scalability is hard; some systems can't process many transactions fast. Environmental issues are also a concern for people, as some coins like Bitcoin need a lot of energy. Their decentralized, semi-anonymous setup raises fear of illegal uses.

Still, the point stands: cryptocurrency offers a secure, decentralized alternative to normal money.

**History of Cryptocurrency**

Money is changing worldwide. Just as we once had a race to the moon, countries now compete to become the crypto capital of the world. To understand this race, we need to look back at the technology that made it all possible. The roots of today's shift reach back to the 1970s, not the 2010s. Back then, cryptography (the science of secure communication) became a formal discipline, not just a secret practice. The era's big step: public-key cryptography, a method that uses two separate codes, a public and a private key, to allow secure communication between people who haven't met. In 1976, Diffie-Hellman solved secure key sharing. A year later, Rivest, Shamir, and Adleman created RSA, enabling public encryption and signatures. At the same time, Data Encryption Standard (DES), an early algorithm for encrypting data became a standard, focusing minds on block ciphers (algorithms that encrypt data in fixed-size chunks) and spurring public analysis. Tools like one-way functions (processes easy to do but hard to undo) and Merkle's puzzles (early cryptographic protocol ideas) set the stage for secure digital systems. This decade saw open research clash with state secrets. The National Security Agency's (NSA) role in DES and export rules limiting encryption are prime examples. Secure web and digital currencies trace their start to these events.

It took decades for these theories to become real technology. In 1988, David Schwartz filed a patent (US5025369A) for a '*multilevel distributed computer system,*' seen by many crypto enthusiasts as an early blockchain. That year, *The Economist* ran *'Get Ready for the Phoenix'* (Jan. 9, 1988). It pictured a future global currency, sparking decades of debate and becoming a widely referenced piece among cryptocurrency fans, who often cite it as evidence of early interest in a borderless, digital financial system.

In the early 2000s, mobile banking rather than cryptocurrency drove major shifts in finance. An article in *Global Finance Magazine*, "*Africa's Mobile Banking: Boom or Bust?*" (2013), shows this shift in action. Kenya's

M-Pesa helped millions transition from cash to digital finance, reshaping local economies and setting a global standard before Bitcoin began to attract wider interest. At that time, Bitcoin was still a niche experiment. In comparison, mobile banking has already had a measurable impact.

What does all this history teach us? Moving value online didn't happen overnight. It's the result of decades of breakthroughs and bold experiments. Do you remember the first time you paid for something online or sent money through an app? That moment was possible thanks to this long journey from early cryptography to today's digital finance revolution.

The rise of cryptocurrency did not happen in isolation. It is part of a much broader technological transformation that is reshaping industries across the world. To understand where digital finance may be heading next, we need to look at the larger wave of innovation now unfolding.

**Emerging Concept (5th Industrial Revolution)**

The Fourth Industrial Revolution (4IR) introduced technologies such as Artificial Intelligence (AI), robotics, and cyber-physical systems, transforming the way we live and work through automation. Machines started doing more of what humans used to do, but they could do it faster and more accurately.

Now, the Fifth Industrial Revolution (5IR) builds on 4IR by highlighting collaboration between advanced technologies and humans. Rather than simply replacing workers, 5IR leverages these tools to enhance human performance, increase productivity, creativity, and innovation. 5IR empowers people, especially in the financial space. Blockchains provide traceability and accountability in transactions, while smart contracts provide a more tamper-proof system, reducing the need to trust intermediaries.

# The Quiet Financial War

Alyssa, a small beauty shop owner, goes to her local bank on Friday to apply for funding to expand. Because the bank has limited Friday hours and the application requires extensive paperwork and review, her request can't be completed before closing. She's told to come back next week, delaying access to the money she needs.

In a different scenario, her competitor Rhianna uses her phone to send a stablecoin transfer, closing a deal within minutes at any time. Hunter, a global freelancer, receives payment in crypto, removing delays and conversion fees. Zak sends money home to his family twice a month and finds cryptocurrencies such as XRP to be a fast, low-cost alternative to traditional remittance services.

Most people tend to ignore financial changes, new technologies, or shifts in the economy until they personally feel the impact (e.g., higher fees, inflation, devaluation, lack of access to better tools). The traditional financial systems (banks, credit cards, wire transfers) may have seemed okay, but now, they feel slow, expensive, or inefficient compared to new options.

There is a major shift happening, a battle. But it is not being widely publicized or understood by the public.

Traditional financial institutions (banks, payment processors) rely on centralized, closed, and often inefficient systems. They act as gatekeepers, deciding who can access certain services and often charging high fees.

Meanwhile, the new financial infrastructure is being built on open, decentralized, blockchain-based systems:

- **Crypto** - cryptocurrencies like Bitcoin, Ethereum, Solana, XRP, etc.
- **Stablecoins** - digital currencies pegged to stable assets (like USDC or USDT)
- **Decentralized Finance (DeFi)** - apps that let people lend, borrow, and trade money directly without needing banks or other intermediaries. These apps use smart contracts, which are self-executing computer programs on the blockchain that automatically carry out financial actions when set conditions are met.

The goal?

Ask yourself: What if moving money could be as easy as sending an email?

Coinbase, the top U.S. centralized exchange, CEO Brian Armstrong has long championed this shift, arguing that crypto ushers in "the age of economic freedom" by expanding access and efficiency, ultimately upgrading the entire financial system. That is the promise of most crypto and precisely why there is fierce pushback. In public debates and recent regulatory proposals, bank-aligned voices are lobbying to restrict exchanges from offering real incentives like competitive yields and instant access instead of the watered-down credit card points we are accustomed to.

Few admit it: today's system hasn't changed much since the 1980s. Apps look new, but processes are old. Bank wire transfer fees range from $15 to $50; some transactions take days and often pause on the weekends. The house got a fresh coat of paint, but the pipes are still rusty.

New rails are rising. Crypto rails that operate 24/7 are permissionless and accessible via smartphone. With stablecoins like USDC, money zips globally in seconds, at 'near-zero cost, without intermediaries. This is not hype! In 2025, the stablecoin market cap surged to nearly $290 billion, powering DeFi protocols and cross-border payments that leave legacy systems in the dust.

It shifts power entirely. When value flows faster, cheaper, and borderless, the old tollbooths (slow settlement times, bank fees, banking hour delays, and approval bottlenecks) start to crumble. A U.S. Treasury report from April 2025 raised a big "what if." What if up to $6.6 trillion in deposits leaves banks over the next 5-7 years and moves into stablecoins that offer better returns? Some stablecoins, such as USDC, can earn 4–10% interest through some crypto exchanges, and decentralized exchanges can be even greater, far more than traditional savings rates of 0.01–4%. Banks are getting worried and pushing back through their lobbyists. The resistance is mounting. Publicly, it is being framed as protecting consumers against scams and instability. These are legitimate concerns. One major example is highlighted by the collapse of Terra in 2022, which wiped out over $40 billion in market value in just a few days. Unlike other stablecoins that are backed by real world assets (RWAs) like U.S. dollars or government bonds, Terra was not supported by anything tangible. Instead, it relied on a second coin, LUNA, to maintain its value through a complex algorithmic model. When that system failed, both coins crashed. Many investors lost a lot of money. Terra's collapse was a catastrophic failure of a unique type of stablecoin known as a non-collateralized algorithmic stablecoin.

Blockchain now brings change to how financial systems work. It allows audits and checks to happen instantly and automatically, making fraud much easier to detect. This helps fix earlier problems found in older financial systems. At its core, this struggle is about control. Traditional systems are adapting. Swift GPI (Global Payments Innovation) now rivals crypto speeds for institutions, and Central Bank Digital Currencies (CBDCs) (e.g. digital yuan) promise to provide fast and efficient payments but with full government oversight and less volatility. Crypto's edge erodes if regulators integrate rails. Banks are not lobbying out of fear alone. The key decision moving forward is weighing permissionless innovation against stability and consumer protection.

The key questions are:

Who owns the system?

Who decides the interest rates?

Who collects the fees?

As an X post captured it: *"Banks know what's coming. Liquidity is shifting. The old guard is crumbling."*

Do you sense we are standing at a crossroads? The signs are everywhere, and the change is real. Are you ready to explore what this new financial world can offer you?

The choice is this: stick with slow, low-return systems, or use always-on, global financial technology. This decision will shape how people and businesses handle money in the future.

It is true that banks desire fast transactions, but only when maintaining control. Cryptocurrency provides fast transfers without requiring approval from intermediaries.

Finance is made to feel dull, keeping us passive. But try sending $1,000 across borders in USDC in 10 seconds for pennies. After seeing that speed, you can't ignore it.

Do you cling to yesterday's slow delays and low returns, or step onto the financial rails designed for an always-on world?

The future is not approaching - it is already here. The only real question is:

***Will you board the new rails?***

# THE LIFE OF BITCOIN

LET'S TALK ABOUT BITCOIN, the most famous cryptocurrency. It is referred to as the world's first "digital gold," acting as a store of value not governed by any government and with a capped supply of 21 million. In 2008, an anonymous person or group using the pseudonym Satoshi Nakamoto published the Bitcoin whitepaper, proposing a peer-to-peer electronic cash system that bypasses financial institutions. The Bitcoin network officially launched in 2009, introducing the world to blockchain, a type of decentralized ledger technology that records every transaction transparently and securely.

Since then, thousands of alternative cryptocurrencies (often called "altcoins") have emerged, each with unique features and use cases. Of course, the crypto world has made huge strides, but it is not perfect. It faces real, ongoing challenges:

- Price volatility
- Complexities of securing your own assets
- The unfortunate reality of scams and fraud
- The risk of losing access through mismanaged private keys
    - Efforts are being made to reduce the need for users to directly manage private keys. Many platforms are introducing systems that abstract key management behind familiar login methods

such as two-factor authentication or single sign-on.

Incidents like Mt. Gox, OneCoin, and FTX have left a stain on the crypto name, damaging trust and leaving a bitter taste in people's mouths just from hearing the word "crypto."

But strangely, these events also did something else. They exposed the flaws that needed fixing. I always try to look at things optimistically, but also realistically. Emerging technologies often go through rough patches in their early stages. Tweaks are needed. Gaps still need to be filled. There are always bugs, missing features, and rough edges just like any version 1.0 product.

I experienced that firsthand when buying the first Xbox and Xbox 360 on release day, only to deal with the infamous "red ring of death." Crypto is no different; growing pains are inevitable, but progress continues.

Here are some additional pivotal moments in the history of cryptocurrency:

- 2009: The Launch of Bitcoin
- 2011: Emergence of altcoins (e.g., Litecoin)
- 2014: The Fall of Mt. Gox exchange
- 2014-2017: OneCoin The Billion-Dollar Illusion
- 2015: Launch of Ethereum, introducing smart contracts
- 2017-2018: Initial Coin Offering (ICO) boom and crypto bubble, followed by a crash
- 2020-2021: DeFi and NFT explosion; growing institutional interest
- 2022: The FTX Collapse: When the King Fell
- 2024-2025: Regulatory advancements, such as the U.S. Clarity Act and the EU's MiCA framework, plus widespread ETF approvals

leading to mainstream adoption.

Much of the hesitation surrounding cryptocurrency still comes from its volatility. Media coverage and government messaging have often amplified fear, uncertainty, and doubt, commonly referred to as FUD within the crypto community.

Despite lingering skepticism, Bitcoin's long-term performance has been extraordinary. After more than 15 years of continuous network operation, BTC has appreciated over 1,000,000 percent since 2009. In July 2025, Bitcoin reached an all-time high of $123,091.61.

This kind of performance has begun reshaping global financial policy. For example, El Salvador adopted Bitcoin as legal tender, marking one of the first times a nation state formally integrated cryptocurrency into its monetary system and signaling its growing role in the global financial landscape.

While Bitcoin proved that decentralized digital money could work without banks or governments, it was only the beginning. Developers soon began asking a bigger question: if blockchain technology could securely record financial transactions, could it also be used to run entire applications and financial systems?

This question led to the next major evolution in the crypto world. In 2015, a new blockchain platform called Ethereum was launched with a different vision. Instead of focusing only on digital currency, Ethereum introduced programmable smart contracts that allowed developers to build decentralized applications directly on the blockchain.

This shift expanded the possibilities of blockchain technology far beyond digital money and opened the door to an entirely new ecosystem of decentralized finance, applications, and digital ownership.

# Beyond Bitcoin: Enter Ethereum

## [No Banks, No Bosses, Just Code]

For years, Bitcoin ruled the crypto world. It proved that money could exist without banks, borders, or intermediaries. But in 2015, a new challenger emerged, one with a bigger dream and not just decentralized money, but a decentralized internet.

Enter Ethereum and, with it, the idea of a world computer.

A young visionary by the name of Vitalik Buterin asked a bold question: If a blockchain can move money, what else can it do? What if it could run programs, power digital communities, and even replace entire industries using only code?

That idea became Ethereum.

Vitalik was not alone. A small group of pioneers joined him:

- Gavin Wood - Wrote the famous *Yellow Paper* and invented Ethereum's programming language Solidity.

- Joseph Lubin, Anthony Di Iorio, Charles Hoskinson, and Mihai Alisie – All co-founders who helped shape the early vision by joining forces to build it.

To fund development, they launched one of the world's first Initial Coin Offerings (ICOs) in 2014. The sale raised over $18 million in Bitcoin, making it one of the largest crowdfunding events of its time.

When Ethereum officially launched in July 2015, it did not just bring digital money; it introduced the world to smart contracts, self-executing code that lives on the blockchain. And with that, the rules of the internet began to change.

**Decentralized Autonomous Organization (DAO) & the First Big Test**

Ethereum's power was clear early on. In 2016, a massive community project called DAO raised over $150 million worth of ETH. It aimed to be a futuristic, leaderless venture fund, governed entirely by smart contracts. But a vulnerability in its code was exploited, and hackers siphoned off over $60 million.

The community faced a defining choice: let the hack stand forever on the blockchain or hard fork the chain to undo the theft and return the stolen funds. In the end, they chose to fork, splitting Ethereum into two versions:

- Ethereum (ETH): the new chain, where the stolen funds were restored.

- Ethereum Classic (ETC): the original chain, where the hack remains in history.

It was a controversial decision, but it set the tone: Ethereum was willing to evolve to protect its community.

**Bitcoin vs. Ethereum: Gold vs. A World Computer**

To understand Ethereum, it helps to compare it to Bitcoin.

Bitcoin - digital gold:

- Purpose: Designed to move and store value without a bank

- Focus: Stability and security above all else
- Like a vault: Strong, reliable, and unchanging
- Limited in supply

Ethereum – global platform:

- Purpose: Designed to build applications
- Focus: Programmability
- Flexible, full of tools, possibilities, and innovation
- Economy: Has its own currency, ETH

Before creating Ethereum, Vitalik Buterin was deeply involved in the early Bitcoin community. He wrote for Bitcoin Magazine, attended Bitcoin meetups, and believed strongly in Bitcoin's potential, but also saw its limitations. Vitalik first suggested making Bitcoin more programmable, but the Bitcoin developers rejected the idea as too risky. So Ethereum was built from scratch as a separate chain focused on programmability. This separation worked:

- Bitcoin remained clean and trusted as "digital gold."
- Ethereum became the world computer, powering experiments in DeFi, NFTs, and DAOs.

Other projects, like Stacks or RSK (Rootstock - a smart contract platform built on top of the Bitcoin blockchain) have tried to bring smart contracts to Bitcoin.

Ethereum remains the epicenter of Web3.

**ERC-20 and The EVM: Ethereum's Secret Weapons**

One of Ethereum's most significant innovations was the ERC-20 standard. Think of it as a universal rulebook for creating new tokens on Ethereum. Before this, launching a cryptocurrency meant building an entirely new blockchain from scratch. With ERC-20, anyone could make a token, tokens for games, fundraising, stablecoins, or even entire new projects with just a few lines of code. This simple standard fueled the ICO boom of 2017 and laid the foundation for today's DeFi and NFT economies.

Powering all of this behind the scenes is the Ethereum Virtual Machine (EVM). The EVM is Ethereum's engine. It is a global computer that runs the same code identically on thousands of nodes around the world. No matter where you are, if you run a smart contract on Ethereum, the EVM makes sure the result is the same everywhere. It is what guarantees fairness, security, and trust. Together, ERC-20 and the EVM turned Ethereum into far more than just digital money. They made it a platform for building entire worlds of value, creativity, and innovation.

**The DeFi Boom: Finance Without Permission**

In 2018, something extraordinary appeared on Ethereum: Uniswap. It looked simple, a place to swap tokens, but under the hood, it was a completely decentralized exchange.

Soon, other DeFi giants arrived:

- Compound and Aave - Allowing anyone to lend, borrow, and earn interest, no credit checks, no gatekeepers, just an internet connection.

- Yearn Finance - Acting like a clever robot-banker, moving funds to wherever it earned the best yield.

The summer of 2020 became legendary as "DeFi Summer." Billions of dollars flooded into smart contracts. People were farming yields, staking tokens, and moving money 24/7; no permission needed.

By the end of 2021, more than $100 billion was locked inside Ethereum's smart contracts. Money was not just sitting in banks anymore; it was moving through code.

And it did not stop with finance. NFTs burst onto the scene, turning digital art, collectibles, and even game items into assets that could be bought, sold, or used as collateral for loans. Ethereum had become both a financial system and a cultural hub, the beating heart of Web3.

Before we go further, it's critical to understand that DeFi's power comes with irreversible risks. Billions have been lost not from hype, but from design realities-automatic, irreversible systems with no built-in safety nets. Let's break this down.

# DeFi Risks and Realities

## DeFi Hacks: Real Risks Beyond the Hype

Decentralized Finance (DeFi) is often marketed as bank-free finance. It is open, permissionless systems where code replaces intermediaries, and users retain full control over their assets. At its peak, DeFi has surpassed $100 billion in total value locked (TVL), enabling lending, trading, and yield generation without traditional banks.

But there is a side of DeFi that rarely gets explained clearly.

Since 2020, over $4 billion has been lost to exploits, hacks, and protocol failures. These losses are not theoretical. They are irreversible. Unlike traditional finance, there is no fraud department, no chargeback, and no emergency rollback.

### Not All Hacks Are the Same

A common misconception is that DeFi hacks are simply the result of "bad code." In reality, most major losses fall into a few repeatable categories.

- Key Management Failures

  The Ronin Network hack in 2022 ($625M) was not caused by a smart contract bug. Attackers used social engineering to compromise validator private keys. Once the keys were exposed, the system worked exactly as designed, just in the attacker's favor.

- Cross-Chain Bridge Vulnerabilities
  Exploits like Poly Network ($611M) and Wormhole ($325M) exposed how bridges dramatically increased risk. Moving assets between blockchains requires complex verification logic, and a single flaw can unlock enormous amounts of value instantly.

- Logic and Economic Exploits
  In many cases, nothing is "broken." Attackers simply find situations the designers didn't anticipate and use them to their advantage.

**The Audit Myth**

A dangerous belief in crypto is that audits solve everything.

They don't.

Roughly 80% of major DeFi exploits occurred on protocols that had already passed audits. Audits reduce risk, but they are point-in-time reviews, not guarantees. Once deployed, a protocol operates in an open, hostile environment that no audit can fully simulate.

**"80% Protection" Is Risk Reduction - Not Insurance**

Some DeFi protocols and coverage providers now advertise up to 80% protection against certain losses. This is a helpful improvement, but it is often misunderstood.

Here's what that protection usually means:

- Coverage applies only to specific failure scenarios (e.g., smart contract exploits, not user error)

- Claims are often capped, delayed, or subject to governance votes

- Payouts may be partial, denominated in tokens, or limited by pool liquidity

- User errors (phishing, wrong addresses, compromised wallets) are almost never covered

In practice, "80% protection" means risk is reduced, not removed.

Platforms like Nexus Mutual are steps in the right direction, but coverage remains optional, incomplete, and unevenly distributed across the ecosystem.

**Immutability Cuts Both Ways**

In traditional finance, reversibility is a feature. In DeFi, immutability is the point.

Once a smart contract is deployed, transactions finalize exactly as written. The blockchain does not distinguish between a mistake and an attack. If funds move, they move permanently.

This is not a temporary flaw or a "growing pain."

It is a structural property of decentralized systems.

**The Real Risk: Responsibility Without a Safety Net**

Self-custody gives users unprecedented control, but also gives unprecedented responsibility.

There is no customer service desk for lost private keys. No authority to reverse transactions. No universal insurance by default. DeFi removes intermediaries and, with them, the safety nets people are used to.

That does not make DeFi broken.
It makes it honest.

The opportunity is real. The innovation is real. And so is the risk.

In DeFi, freedom and responsibility are inseparable.

The system will not save you from your mistakes or from someone else's.

# Ethereum Today

### Ethereum's Challenges

Like any rapidly evolving technology, Ethereum faces several challenges. High gas fees and network congestion can make transactions expensive during periods of heavy demand. The system is also complex for new users, requiring an understanding of wallets, tokens, and private keys.

Although Ethereum dramatically reduced its environmental footprint after the 2022 Merge, critics still debate the long-term implications of proof-of-stake and whether large validators could accumulate influence. At the same time, competing networks such as Solana, Avalanche, and BNB Chain continue pushing for faster and cheaper alternatives.

Despite all this, Ethereum's ecosystem remains the most vibrant.

### The Heart of the Movement

Ethereum isn't perfect. Its roads get clogged, its tolls are high, and its rivals circle hungrily. But it remains the place where the most innovative experiments happen, from decentralized banks to digital art markets. ETH remains the most famous when referring to developers and the DeFi market. Developers are building Layer 2 solutions like Arbitrum, Optimism, and Base to reduce fees and boost speed. Future upgrades like sharding will increase capacity to serve billions of users.

Where Bitcoin gave us digital money, Ethereum gave us a digital economy. Ethereum's story was not perfect, but it remains the heart of a movement that promises freedom, creativity, and open finance for the world.

It is not just a blockchain. It is a movement built on a promise: no banks, no bosses, just code.

# Web3 and the New Digital Economy

### Understanding Web3

To grasp how Web3 is transforming the internet, it's helpful first to understand the evolution from Web 1.0 through Web 2.0. Each era changed not only how we access information, but how we interact, share, and now, exchange value online.

Think of this as your come-to-Jesus, *Buddha, Allah, or Tom Cruise moment*" … whichever inspires you most.

**Web 1.0** – *The Letter Era*

This was the read-only internet.

Imagine the days when sending a message meant writing a letter. It could take 3–14 days to reach someone, depending on the distance. Then, along came email. Suddenly, your computer would say, "You've got mail!" and your message would be delivered instantly. You could visit websites and read information, but you could not interact much.

**Web 2.0** – *The Social Era*

Now, imagine the same leap forward for sharing larger amounts of data. Before sending videos, large amounts of data, or photos, it could take a day or hours to download or transfer. With Web 2.0, platforms like

Facebook, Instagram, and video chat made sharing massive amounts of information nearly instant. You could send large files, stream videos, video calls, and share globally without delays.

**Web 3.0 –** *The Money/Ownership Era*

Now the game-changer arrives.

Web 3.0 integrates finance directly into the fabric of the internet. In the past, sending money, getting a refund, or transferring value required banks and could take days. Now, with Web 3.0, financial transactions and ownership are instant, global, and decentralized, powered by blockchain, cryptocurrencies, and smart contracts. Money and assets move as quickly and seamlessly as information did in earlier eras.

## The New Financial Infrastructure

### Expanding Beyond Currency

The crypto ecosystem is no longer limited to just currency or speculation; it now spans nearly every sector, powering a wide range of innovations and real-world applications. Understanding its structure and interconnections is essential for anyone navigating or investing in digital assets. Here's an overview of the current landscape and why it matters.

The crypto market has rapidly expanded into nearly every industry. While much attention goes to banking and finance, blockchain technology also powers innovations in gaming, stock trading, real-world asset tokenization (RWAs), NFTs & digital collectibles and power generation. Looking ahead, blockchains will secure healthcare data, streamline supply chains, and enable digital ID systems for voting, travel, and universal verification (AI vs. human), unlocking new levels of security and ownership.

### Blockchain Architecture and Layers

Blockchain systems are often described in layers, much like the architecture of the internet. Each layer serves a different purpose, working together to support decentralized networks and the applications built on top of them. These layers help organize how data is transmitted, validated, and used across blockchain ecosystems.

Understanding these layers makes it easier to see how different networks interact and how new technologies continue to expand what blockchain systems can do.

### Layer 0 Blockchains

Layer 0 refers to the foundational infrastructure that allows different blockchains to communicate and operate together. It focuses on the underlying protocols that connect networks, enabling interoperability and shared communication between multiple chains.

Rather than hosting applications directly, Layer 0 provides the base environment that supports the creation and interaction of various blockchain networks. It helps solve the challenge of blockchains operating in isolation by allowing them to exchange information and assets more efficiently.

### Layer 1

Layer 1 blockchains are the primary networks where transactions are recorded and validated. These are the base protocols that maintain the core ledger, handle consensus mechanisms, and secure the network.

Well-known Layer 1 systems include networks like Bitcoin and Ethereum. These blockchains process transactions directly on their own networks and serve as the foundation for many applications and services in the crypto ecosystem.

**Examples of Layer 1 Blockchains:**

- **Ethereum (ETH):** The second-largest cryptocurrency and the dominant platform for smart contracts, dApps, and DeFi.
- **Binance Coin (BNB):** The native coin of the BNB Chain, a popular network known for its speed and low transaction fees.
- **Solana (SOL):** Known for its high transaction speed and low costs, making it a favorite for NFTs and Web3 gaming.
- **Ripple (XRP):** The native token of the XRP Ledger is focused on fast, low-cost international payments. They also have a stable coin named RLUSD
- **Cardano (ADA):** A blockchain platform known for its research-driven, peer-reviewed development approach.
- **Sui (SUI):** A newer layer 1 blockchain built by ex-Meta engineers, attracting attention for its speed and scalability.
- **Avalanche (AVAX):** A high-performance, scalable platform for dApps and custom blockchains.

**Layer 2**

As blockchain networks grew in popularity, many began facing a major challenge: scalability. When too many transactions compete for space on the main blockchain, processing times slow down and transaction fees increase.

Layer 2 solutions were developed to help address this problem. Instead of processing every transaction directly on the main blockchain, Layer 2 systems handle much of the activity off-chain while still relying on the underlying network for security.

By moving some transaction activity away from the primary chain and settling the final results back onto it later, Layer 2 technologies can dramatically increase transaction speed while reducing costs for users.

Several Layer 2 platforms have emerged to help scale blockchain networks such as Ethereum. Examples include systems like Arbitrum, Optimism, and Polygon, which allow decentralized applications to operate more efficiently while maintaining compatibility with the broader Ethereum ecosystem.

**Rollups**

Rollups are one of the most important Layer 2 scaling approaches. They work by grouping many transactions together off the main blockchain and then submitting a compressed version of those transactions back to the primary network. This allows the system to process far more activity without overwhelming the base chain.

Even though most of the computation happens off-chain, the final transaction data is still recorded on the underlying blockchain, which preserves security and transparency. Rollups are often used to help scale networks such as Ethereum by increasing throughput while keeping the benefits of the main chain's security.

**Sidechains**

Sidechains represent another approach to improving blockchain scalability. A sidechain is a separate blockchain that runs alongside a main network but remains connected to it through bridging mechanisms.

Because sidechains operate independently, they can process transactions using their own rules and consensus mechanisms. This allows them to offer faster transactions and lower fees while still interacting with the broader blockchain ecosystem.

Several blockchain networks have experimented with sidechain architectures to support specialized applications such as gaming, decentralized finance, and enterprise solutions.

**Layer 3**

Layer 3 represents the application layer where users interact with blockchain technology through various platforms and services. This is where decentralized applications, financial tools, and digital services are built.

While the lower layers focus on infrastructure and network performance, Layer 3 focuses on usability and real-world applications. It allows developers to create products that people can use directly, from decentralized finance platforms to digital identity systems and online marketplaces.

# DeFi and Financial Infrastructure

### From Infrastructure to Financial Applications

While the lower layers of blockchain architecture focus on network security, scalability, and data processing, the application layer is where these technologies begin to transform real-world systems. Once the underlying infrastructure is in place, developers can build platforms that replicate and improve many of the services traditionally provided by banks, exchanges, and financial institutions.

One of the most significant developments to emerge from this layered blockchain architecture is decentralized finance, commonly known as DeFi. By using smart contracts and decentralized networks, DeFi platforms attempt to recreate financial services such as lending, trading, and payments without relying on centralized intermediaries.

But finance is only one part of the story.

As blockchain infrastructure matured, developers began applying the same technology to entirely new industries. Gaming, artificial intelligence, social platforms, and data networks are now building their own decentralized ecosystems on top of blockchain foundations.

These emerging sectors represent the next phase of the crypto economy, where blockchain moves beyond money and begins reshaping entire digital industries.

In the following sections, we explore several of the most important sectors currently emerging in the blockchain space.

# Emerging Blockchain Sectors

## Self-Sovereign Identity

As digital systems evolve, identity is becoming just as important as money. In a world where transactions, services, and interactions are increasingly automated, the question is no longer just *what you own*, but *who you are in the system*.

Traditionally, identity has been managed by institutions. Banks, governments, and platforms store and verify personal information, acting as intermediaries for access and trust. But this model creates friction, privacy risks, and dependency on centralized systems.

Self-sovereign identity offers a different approach. Instead of relying on institutions to hold and verify identity, individuals control their own credentials, deciding what to share, when to share it, and with whom. These credentials can be secured and verified using blockchain-based systems, allowing identity to be portable, tamper-resistant, and independently validated.

In this model, a wallet evolves beyond a place to store assets. It becomes an identity layer. Holding not just financial value, but credentials, permissions, and proofs. Access to services, platforms, and transactions can be granted through cryptographic verification rather than institutional approval.

This shift becomes even more important as AI agents begin acting on behalf of users. An AI agent making a purchase, negotiating a contract, or interacting with a marketplace must be able to prove authorization. Self-sovereign identity enables this by linking the agent's actions to verifiable credentials controlled by the user.

Projects such as Jasmy, an application-layer token built on Ethereum (ERC-20), are exploring models where individuals own their personal data and grant access as needed, rather than surrendering it to centralized platforms. In this framework, data becomes an asset, one that can be secured, shared selectively, and used by AI systems operating under the user's control.

Without this foundation, automated systems introduce new risks. Disputes over transactions, unauthorized actions, and data misuse become more difficult to resolve. With it, identity becomes verifiable, portable, and programmable. Enabling trust in a digital, automated economy.

As financial systems evolve, identity and value begin to converge. The same infrastructure that allows money to move without intermediaries may also allow identity to function the same way. Secure, user-controlled, and globally accessible.

**Blockchain AI**

The convergence of blockchain and artificial intelligence (AI) is set to transform both industries, creating a new layer of intelligent, automated, and secure financial services. Here's how these two powerful technologies are working together, and why it matters for the future:

Imagine waking up and discovering your financial life is running itself. Your AI assistant isn't just monitoring crypto markets; it's actively managing your money, paying bills, and making purchases for you securely and transparently, thanks to blockchain technology.

Need dinner? Instead of scrolling through DoorDash, AI already knows your dietary preferences, dietary restrictions, and weekly budget. It places the order, pays instantly using your crypto wallet, and all you get is a notification when the food arrives.

Planning a trip? Your AI scans flights across airlines, compares hotel options, books the best combination, and automatically completes payment using blockchain-based transactions. No middlemen, no hidden fees, just instant, auditable payments.

Shopping for clothes? AI analyzes your style and size, finds items you will like, and even negotiates prices with online retailers. Payment is handled seamlessly, and the receipt is stored securely on the blockchain for proof of purchase.

This is where AI meets blockchain in everyday life. AI provides personalization and decision-making, while blockchain delivers security, data ownership, and transparency. Together, they build an intelligent, automated financial layer woven into your daily routines.

Zooming out, AI not only manages your DeFi portfolio, optimizing trades, earning yield, and securing assets, but also handles your daily needs like food, travel, shopping, and subscriptions. All of this is powered by smart contracts: self-executing code on the blockchain that automates tasks without requiring trust in a third party.

The result? A world where money doesn't just sit in your account, it works for you. Your AI determines when to spend, save, invest, or adapt to the market. Every transaction flows through blockchain rails, making finance seamless, secure, transparent, and user-owned.

This future isn't science fiction, it's the next evolutionary step. AI becomes your digital concierge, while blockchain acts as the trusted, tamper-proof record-keeper. Together, they pave the way for automated, intelligent, and accessible financial freedom.

### Oracles and Interoperability Protocols

Most blockchains are like islands. They can run programs and store data, but they do not naturally connect to the outside world or even to each other. That is where oracles and interoperability protocols come in. They are the bridges and messengers that connect blockchains to real-world data, such as weather, prices, sports scores, and more, as well as connecting different blockchains.

Think of oracles as the "eyes and ears" of a blockchain. On their own, smart contracts can only access the data that is already stored on-chain. Without outside information, they would be blind and unaware of the price of ETH in U.S. dollars, the weather in your city, or the score of last night's basketball game. Oracles solve this problem by securely delivering off-chain data to smart contracts, enabling blockchain applications to perform useful tasks. For example, DeFi apps rely on price feeds from oracles to facilitate lending, borrowing, and trading. Insurance protocols use weather data from oracles to automatically pay claims after storms or natural disasters.

To ensure reliability and prevent manipulation, decentralized oracle networks, such as Chainlink, pull data from multiple sources and utilize cryptographic proofs to verify accuracy. This builds trust because no single source controls the data, significantly reducing the risk of false or biased information entering the system.

In short, oracles are how blockchains "talk" to the real world. Without them, smart contracts could not respond to external events, rendering many blockchain applications, such as lending, insurance, or prediction markets, impossible. Oracles take blockchains beyond simply recording data, enabling them to interact with the world around us.

### SocialFi & The Creator Economy

SocialFi (Social Finance) and the Creator Economy are redefining how value, ownership, and influence are distributed online. These blockchain-powered platforms empower users and creators to monetize their content, build communities, and participate in the upside of their social engagement, transforming the internet from an attention economy to an ownership economy.

Let's be real, traditional social media is a bit of a raw deal. You post, scroll, send, and share all day, but the platforms make most of the money. They harvest your data, flood your feed with ads, and only the top 1% of creators see any real income. Everyone else is just giving away their time and attention for free.

SocialFi flips this model on its head. Instead of platforms owning your content and pocketing the profits, blockchain-based SocialFi platforms share value with users and creators. Participants can earn tokens, gain ownership stakes, and have a real say in how the platform evolves.

Here's how it works: Users earn tokens by posting quality content, curating communities, or actively engaging with others. Creators can launch personal tokens or mint NFTs tied to their work, while fans who support them unlock perks like exclusive content, early access, or even community voting rights. In this way, fans become stakeholders in the creator's success

The big shift is ownership and portability. On SocialFi, your profile and data belong to you, making it possible to move your digital identity between platforms. Community governance replaces top-down algorithms, giving users a voice in how platforms grow and what content is prioritized.

Projects like Friend.tech, Zora, and DeSo are leading the way in experimenting with SocialFi models, attracting attention from major investors such as Coinbase Ventures. This signals that SocialFi is gaining momentum as a serious evolution of online social platforms.

Challenges remain, including token volatility, evolving regulations, and user experience hurdles that still need to be addressed. Yet the potential is massive: SocialFi transforms the attention economy into an ownership economy, sharing value among creators, users, and communities rather than concentrating profits with platforms.

SocialFi is setting the stage for a fairer, more engaging, and more rewarding online experience where likes, shares, and participation translate into real value for everyone involved.

**Blockchain Gaming**

Blockchain gaming is reshaping the traditional video game industry by offering actual digital ownership, new earning opportunities, and cross-game interoperability. Here's how blockchain is transforming the gaming world and why it matters for players and developers alike:

Think about the last time you played a video game. Maybe you spent hours unlocking a rare weapon or even paid for an exclusive skin. It felt valuable, right? Here is the catch: you do not actually own it. The game company does. If the servers shut down tomorrow, you will lose all those items you worked for.

This is why gaming and blockchain fit together so naturally. With blockchain, players truly own their digital assets, such as weapons, skins, or rare collectibles, as tokens on a decentralized ledger. Early projects like Axie Infinity popularized the "play-to-earn" model, allowing players to earn real-world value for their in-game achievements.

The next evolution is interoperability. Blockchain enables digital assets and identities to move between different games and platforms, breaking down barriers between virtual worlds. Imagine bringing a rare sword from one game into another or using your avatar across multiple metaverse experiences.

This also connects to E-sports (sports betting) and the metaverse. E-sports already moves billions of dollars, but blockchain could make things even bigger. Secure prize pools, fan ownership of teams, and massive virtual arenas where tournaments feel like entire cities are built online.

Major companies like Microsoft, Sony, Nintendo, and SEGA are exploring blockchain integrations. Imagine designing a custom weapon in a popular game, minting it as an NFT (non-fungible token), and trading or selling it across platforms, earning royalties each time it changes hands. This is the future of gaming: player-driven economies powered by actual digital ownership.

It is not only about gaming consoles anymore. Solana, a major blockchain, already launched its own smartphone, The Seeker, priced around $500. Pair it with Helium's blockchain-powered mobile network and you get unlimited calls, texts, and data for about $30 per month, plus crypto rewards that can offset the cost. Early buyers of the phone even received airdrops that sometimes covered the price of the phone itself. Plus, the phone comes with special blockchain apps you cannot get anywhere else. Some of these apps even pay you just for walking or running. So, your phone might soon earn you money just for being active.

In summary, blockchain gaming is not just about entertainment; it's about owning your items, earning as you play, and participating in vibrant digital economies that connect the virtual and real worlds. In this new landscape, players are empowered as stakeholders, not just consumers.

**Top gaming coins (as of mid-2025)**

**Immutable (IMX) -** Layer-2 for NFTs and blockchain gaming.
**Floki (FLOKI)** – Meme-inspired token with gaming utilities.
**Gala (GALA)** – Ecosystem powering a range of play-to-earn games.
**The Sandbox (SAND) -** Virtual world creation and monetization platform.
**Decentraland (MANA)**– Metaverse focused on user-generated content.
**Axie Infinity (AXS)**– Battle and collect creatures to earn crypto.
**Wemix (WEMIX)**– Platform for decentralized apps and games.
**Ronin (RON)**– Sidechain optimized for high-performance gaming.

**Notcoin (NOT)**– Tap-to-earn simple gaming token.

**Illuvium (ILV)** – NFT-based world of exploration and strategic battles.

# The Engines Powering the System

**Energy: The Hidden Layer of the New Financial World**

Every digital system ultimately runs on one thing: energy. Blockchains, cryptocurrencies, data centers, and artificial intelligence are often described as "digital," but there is nothing abstract about their foundations. Every transaction, smart contract, AI model, or prompt is powered by electricity flowing through real, physical infrastructure. In this sense, energy is the real base layer of the modern economy.

**Why Blockchain, Crypto, and AI Need Energy**

Blockchain uses energy to keep networks secure, process transactions, and maintain decentralization. Bitcoin, in particular, converts electricity into security. Miners compete to solve cryptographic puzzles that protect the network. Newer blockchain systems use far less power, but they still depend on continuous electricity to keep validators online and data flowing.

Crypto markets never sleep. Exchanges, wallets, and trading systems operate 24/7, meaning any power disruption creates immediate risk. AI takes this even further. Training large models or running real-time AI systems can consume as much electricity as a small city. Without reliable energy, the digital economy stops entirely.

### From Energy Users to Energy Innovators

Here's what makes this moment different: blockchain and AI don't just consume energy, they can reshape how it's produced, financed, and paid for. From my perspective, nuclear energy fits this new model better than almost any other source. It delivers massive, always-on power with near-zero emissions, making it uniquely suited for energy-hungry systems like AI data centers and industrial-scale digital infrastructure.

The challenge isn't technology, it's policy. In many regions, regulatory uncertainty, long approval timelines, and shifting political rules make nuclear projects look less attractive from an investment standpoint, even when the underlying economics are strong. Capital isn't afraid of nuclear energy; it's afraid of decades of regulatory risk being layered on top of it.

Japan offers a useful example. It has taken a more integrated approach by pairing nuclear power with large-scale hydrogen production, treating excess clean energy as a resource rather than wasted capacity. That approach has helped Japan reduce reliance on fossil fuels while positioning as a global leader in hydrogen and fuel-cell technology, led by companies like Toyota.

### Tokenizing Power Plants (The Big Idea)

Imagine a modern gas power plant divided into digital tokens. Each token represents a share of its electricity output, revenue, or even carbon credits. As the plant generates power, smart software automatically distributes payments to token holders.

This model isn't widespread yet. Regulation still needs to catch up, but the concept is powerful. The same approach applies to solar farms, wind turbines, grid-scale batteries, waste-to-energy facilities, and even future small nuclear reactors. Energy shifts from being rigid and exclusive to something liquid and accessible.

### Miners Becoming Power Pioneers

Bitcoin miners are leading this transition.

They learned early how to secure cheap electricity, negotiate with utilities, and operate energy-intensive infrastructure. Now, many are repurposing mining sites into AI and data centers. Same locations, same power access, different machines.

When the grid is stressed, mining can pause and release power back. When electricity is abundant, AI workloads ramp up. What critics once called "wasted energy" is increasingly recognized as flexible demand that helps stabilize the grid while supporting the AI boom.

### Governments Push Data Centers to Generate Power

Governments are starting to respond. AI data centers now draw power more like factories than office buildings. Regulators are sending a clear message: if companies want massive campuses pulling hundreds of megawatts, they may need to supply their own electricity.

Expect data centers to be built next to power generation-gas, wind, solar, hydro, and eventually small modular reactors. These facilities will fund their own substations, secure long-term energy contracts, or generate power on-site. Data centers are no longer just energy customers; they are becoming energy partners.

### AI Makes Energy Smarter

AI ties the system together.

With real-time energy data, AI can predict demand, balance supply, route electricity efficiently, and reduce waste and downtime. Blockchain manages trust, ownership, and payments. AI handles optimization and decision-making. Energy becomes a dynamic system that improves continuously.

**Real Companies Are Already Doing This**

This isn't science fiction. Major organizations are already exploring how blockchain and AI can reshape energy markets and infrastructure. Shell has studied blockchain for energy trading, settlement, and operational transparency. Peer-reviewed research published by MDPI analyzes how tokenization can improve efficiency and financing, and coordination across energy systems. Platforms like RWA.io focus on tokenizing real-world assets, such as power plants and grid infrastructure. Enterprise strategists at GEP analyze how tokenization could modernize oil, gas, and industrial energy supply chains.

The pattern is consistent: when power becomes scarce and capital tightens, serious players turn to digital infrastructure for solutions.

**The Real Bottom Line**

The internet changed how we share information.

Blockchain is changing how we move value.

AI is changing how decisions are made.

Energy makes all three real.

The next winners won't just build apps or chase tokens. They'll control the power that runs everything. In the coming decade, kilowatt-hours may matter as much as dollars. Those who understand this early will see opportunity where others see limits.

The physical infrastructure behind blockchain and AI may power the system, but infrastructure alone doesn't explain how the crypto economy behaves.

Unlike traditional financial systems, where banks, exchanges, and regulators tightly control when and how money moves, crypto markets operate on open networks that never close. These systems react instantly to global events, new technology, and shifts in investor sentiment.

To understand why crypto markets rise, fall, and sometimes move with extreme volatility, we need to look at how this new digital financial system actually functions.

# How the Crypto Economy Works

**Why the Crypto Market Moves the Way It Does**

Many people still don't understand why the crypto market is as volatile as it is. They try to compare it to the stock market, but the two are built on entirely different systems.

In the stock market, major movements usually happen around predictable events, such as quarterly earnings reports, central bank announcements, or policy changes. These reports come every few months, and while news or speculation can cause small shifts, there's often a lag before the broader market reacts. Traditional finance moves on schedules, procedures, and closed trading hours.

Crypto doesn't.

The cryptocurrency market runs in real time, 24 hours a day, 7 days a week. There are no closing bells or weekends off. When global news breaks, when a new regulation passes, or when a major wallet moves billions of dollars, the market responds immediately. Prices adjust within minutes or hours, not weeks.

This constant activity is why crypto's volatility can feel extreme. It reflects an open, borderless system reacting to live global sentiment. There's no waiting to "see what happens." Information flows nonstop, and the market digests it just as fast.

This is also why legacy financial systems struggle to keep pace. They were built for delayed settlement, regulated hours, and centralized control. Crypto, on the other hand, operates like the internet: global, instant, and always on.

# Institutional Adoption

### Top Investors of Crypto

The game has changed. Behind the scenes, some of the world's largest investors and companies are buying large amounts of Bitcoin and Ethereum (ETH), the two most well-known cryptocurrencies. They seem to share one key understanding: crypto, especially Bitcoin, is becoming a long-term store of value. It is something to hold to protect your wealth over time, like gold.

| Name | Company | Notable Holdings |
|---|---|---|
| Michael Saylor | MicroStrategy | 240,000+ BTC |
| Elon Musk | Tesla/SpaceX | Combined corporate: 19,788 BTC ($1.8 billion) |
| Raoul Pal | Real Vision | BTC, ETH, XRP, SOL, SUI |
| Cathie Wood | ARK Invest | 25% of net worth in BTC, ARK's ARKB ETF: 43,740.5 BTC (as of Sept. 11, 2025) |
| Tom Lee | BitMine | Over 2 million ETH ($9.2 billion, largest corporate holder) |
| Donald Trump | World Liberty Financial | The family's total crypto-related wealth exceeds $6 billion, with at least $500 million in confirmed realized earnings to date. (Sept 2025) [1] |

## Top Government Bitcoin Holdings

| Country | BTC Holdings | Approximate Value (USD) | Acquisition Method | Source Info |
|---|---|---|---|---|
| USA | 198,112 | $22.2 billion | Primarily from criminal seizures, including the Silk Road marketplace and the Bitfinex hack. On-chain data confirms this despite FOIA queries on US Marshal's' control. | Binance.com<br>CNN.com<br>Coinpedia.org<br>Finance.yahoo.com<br>Coingecko.com |
| China | 190,000 | $21.09 billion | Seized from fraudulent schemes like PlusToken, despite a national ban on crypto trading. Some sources note the original seizure was 194,775 BTC, with uncertainty on current holdings.<br>(The ban was lifted in 2025) | Visualcapitalist.com<br>Coinpedia.com<br>Coingecko.com<br>Paxful.com |
| United Kingdom | 61,245 | $6.80 billion | Largely from donations supporting defense and humanitarian efforts amid ongoing conflicts. Recent legalization efforts (e.g., new tax bill in September 2025) aim to regulate crypto but don't indicate sales of holdings. | Coinpedia.com<br>Coingecko.com<br>Paxful.com<br>Ccn.com |
| Ukraine | >46,351 | $5.14 billion | Largely from donations supporting defense and humanitarian efforts amid ongoing conflicts. Recent legalization efforts (e.g., new tax bill in September 2025) aim to regulate crypto but don't indicate sales of holdings. | Thecryptobasic.com<br>Coinpedia.com<br>Coingecko.com<br>Paxful.com |
| Bhutan | >10,000 | $1.17 billion | Accumulated via secretive mining operations powered by hydroelectric energy; occasional sales (e.g., $59 in July 2025) to manage reserves, but holdings remain substantial. | Coinpedia.org<br>Coingecko.com<br>Paxful.com<br>Ccn.com<br>Cryptoninjas.net<br>Finance.yahoo.com |
| El Salvador | >6,000 | $0.70 billion | Strategic purchases as part of adopting BTC as legal tender to bolster national finances, including ongoing buys; recently split holdings across multiple addresses for security (e.g., against quantum threats) as of late August 2025. | Thecryptobasic.com<br>Coinpedia.com<br>Coingecko.com<br>Paxful.com<br>Crystalintelligence.com |

Let's talk about Mainland China. The policy regarding cryptocurrency is very strict. Since 2021, the People's Bank of China (PBOC) and regulators have made it illegal to operate crypto exchanges or trade digital assets on the mainland. They also banned crypto mining, which is a process used to create new coins like Bitcoin. Technically, owning crypto is not illegal, but you cannot legally buy, sell, or trade it through platforms based in China.

Instead, the Chinese government's focus is on building its own state-backed digital currency, called the digital yuan (e-CNY). This central bank digital currency (CBDC) is fully controlled and issued by the government, enabling high levels of monitoring and control over money movement.

When you see claims that "China owns a lot of Bitcoin," they usually refer to coins seized by police from scams like the PlusToken case. Those coins were confiscated, not purchased for a reserve or investment strategy. Authorities typically sell off these seized assets through legal processes. This is very different than making a strategic buy to hold them as part of their national reserves.

Hong Kong takes a much different approach. State-linked financial firms now offer regulated Bitcoin and Ethereum ETFs (exchange-traded funds) and custody services (secure storage for crypto assets). This means investors can gain crypto exposure through Hong Kong, but it does not mean Mainland China is officially investing in Bitcoin. Also, some Chinese state-owned banks have branches in Hong Kong that provide accounts or services to regulated crypto firms.

As of 2025, the total global government holdings of Bitcoin are estimated at around 463,000 - 527,000 BTC, which is roughly 2.2% - 2.5% of its supply.

Let's look at what is happening in America.

Traditional savings accounts are losing value because their returns often do not keep up with inflation. This means the purchasing power of your dollars shrinks as the years go by.  Meanwhile, assets like crypto redefine wealth and growth. Let's take an example:

In 2017, the average home price was about $225,000. At the time, Bitcoin's all-time high was $19,000, so you would have needed 11.84 BTC to buy that home.

In 2025, that same home now costs about $400,000.

But with Bitcoin reaching an ATH of $123,000+, you would now need only 3.25 BTC to purchase it.

This shift highlights a bigger truth:

While the dollar loses value over time, specific cryptocurrencies, especially Bitcoin, continue to appreciate significantly.

# The Future of Finance

**Why This Matters for the Future of Finance**

The rapid evolution of blockchain, digital assets, and decentralized finance (DeFi) isn't just a technological trend; it's reshaping the very foundation of the global financial system. Understanding why this matters is crucial for anyone aiming to navigate, participate in, or benefit from the next era of financial innovation.

There are specific key financial blockchains being built to become the backbone of global finance and money movement. In the near future, many mainstream banks, payment systems, and fintech apps are expected to operate on these blockchain "rails." Here are some concepts to understand:

**Gas Fees**

Most Layer 1 blockchains (like Ethereum, Solana, etc.) require a small fee to process transactions. Whenever you transfer assets between wallets, you will need to pay these fees. This is how the network compensates for the computing power required to process your transaction. Some exchanges waive transaction fees in exchange for a subscription service.

Let's break it down with an analogy. Imagine driving a diesel truck. You cannot fill it up with regular ethanol gas and expect it to run correctly. You need the correct fuel at the pump, or your car will have problems.

Cryptocurrency works the same way. Each blockchain uses a specific type of "fuel" (its own coin or native token) to run transactions. If you are using Ethereum, you will need ETH as gas. If you are using Solana, you will need S OL.

When setting up a new wallet, especially a decentralized one, you are in charge. You will usually need to provide this "fuel" yourself to pay for transactions. And when transferring coins, tokens, or NFTs, it is crucial to select the correct blockchain. In cases where the native coin is not available, some platforms provide wrapped tokens as alternatives. Sending a coin to the wrong chain can result in it being lost permanently.

So, what exactly does "wrapped" mean? Here is an example:

Let's use a Florida reference. Picture a saltwater fish like a snook. The snook represents XRP (an altcoin), while the XRP Ledger is the saltwater, its natural environment. Now, imagine moving that snook into a freshwater lake, which represents a different blockchain, like Base. If you drop it in, it will not survive. But if you put the snook in a special "saltwater suit," it can live in a freshwater lake while still being a saltwater fish.

That is what a wrapped token does. It allows an asset to exist and function in a different blockchain ecosystem without losing its identity. In this case, the wrapped version of XRP on the Base blockchain is called cbXRP, and this means you can purchase and use XRP within Base, even though its native "waters" are elsewhere.

**Interoperability**

Currently, many blockchains operate in silo. Interoperability refers to the ability for different blockchains to communicate and transfer value seamlessly. Just like Visa, Mastercard, and PayPal networks connect banks globally, future financial blockchains will need to connect so assets can move freely between ecosystems. Projects are already building the tools to connect all these blockchains into one big ecosystem, including:

- Polkadot – Multichain network
- Quant Overledger - A layer 2.0 solution connecting enterprise and retail systems
- Cosmos – Internet of blockchains.

**Liquidity**

Decentralized exchanges (DEXs) like Uniswap or PancakeSwap need liquidity to function correctly. More liquidity means having enough assets in a pool to allow users to buy, sell, or swap tokens without big price swings. Essentially, more liquidity means better prices, less slippage, and faster transactions. As big players (like investment firms and banks) move into crypto, their demand will drive liquidity and strengthen these platforms.

## The Transformation of Banking

### Rethink Traditional Banking

Now ask yourself:

*Has your bank account grown by 30% in six months?* Probably not.

Traditional banking is now coming to a crossroads. As I mentioned earlier, banks must evolve with new technology and offer high-yield returns. Banks may have to change how they operate, even paying customers to take a loan just to be competitive. It may sound unbelievable, but it is already happening in some places. If banks do not adapt, they could end up like Blockbuster –left behind.

The point is:

If DeFi can grow your money faster than a savings account, why keep it in a system that is not fighting inflation? That is the key takeaway. You want your money to grow, not lose value over time. Leaving your income in a traditional fiat account is not going to keep you ahead in this rapidly evolving financial landscape.

Wealth-minded individuals and investors do not let their money sit idle. They understand:

- Inflation erodes the value of money
- The cost of living, especially housing, keeps rising
- Multiple streams of income are no longer a luxury; they are a necessity

Having a job or career as a source of income is essential, but creating recurring income from strategic investments is how people stay ahead. This is one of the easiest ways to generate a second income without physical labor, leaving your house, purchasing equipment, or relying on others to provide an opportunity or dependable help. You will not become a millionaire overnight. But with time and effort, you can be better off each year than the last. Yes, there is always risk. It is even higher when you do not fully understand what you are doing. We have years of crypto data behind it, and the market is only just starting to grow again. If you invest smart, the right amount, at the right time, in the right place, it could be life-changing.

Meanwhile, as major geopolitical events (like rising tensions between countries) dominate headlines, many people miss the significant financial changes that are happening quietly behind the scenes. In the same timeframe, several important U.S. financial and crypto-related bills were quietly passed, including:

**As of 2025:**

| Bill | Role in the Stack | What it Changes |
|---|---|---|
| FIT21 (Financial Innovation and Technology for the 21st Century Act) | Market Structure & Lanes | Defines when a token/network is a digital commodity (CFTC oversight) vs. a security (SEC oversight); establishes venue rules, disclosures, and regulatory divisions between SEC and CFTC. |
| CLARITY Act (Digital Asset Market Clarity Act, formerly referred to as Securities Clarity Act) | Definition Fix | Clarifies that a token sold via an investment contract isn't itself a security by default; provides pathways for tokens to transition to commodities upon decentralization. |
| GENIUS Act (Guiding and Establishing National Innovation for U.S. Stablecoins Act) | Payment Rails | Creates a federal framework for fiat-backed stablecoins, requiring 1:1 reserves with high-quality assets, redemption rights, bankruptcy priority for holders, AML/consumer protections, and issuer eligibility for banks/nonbanks |
| CBDC Anti-Surveillance State Act | Guardrail | Prohibits the Federal Reserve from issuing a retail CBDC without explicit congressional authorization; restricts any potential CBDC to protect privacy and prevent surveillance. |

**The Broader Financial Sector**

You may feel like you do not have enough money to get involved, especially when hearing the cost of one Bitcoin (BTC). But here is the truth:

It is not about how much money you have; it is about where you start investing.

There are entry points for every budget. For example:

In February 2025, I opened a crypto account and received $5.00 in BTC when the price was over $80,000. By August, that same $5.00 grew to $6.53, a 30.53% increase in just six months.

Yes, prices can go back down. But with the power of DeFi, it can also be converted to USDC or any other stablecoin and earn a yield or rewards. Some decentralized platforms offer as high as **23% APR,** though most average around 4-9% APR. And "*YES*", since it is a stablecoin, the price remains stable at one dollar. Stablecoins are not as volatile! You can also withdraw it at any time or move it back to a regular ACH account. That is a larger deep dive into the capabilities of cryptocurrency and is a little more advanced. But before long, you will not need to exchange stablecoins at all. They will be accepted everywhere. Mastercard and Visa are already on board, also offering crypto rewards. You may have already seen some Bitcoin ATMs. Soon, the payment terminals from grocery stores to gas stations will be upgraded to handle diverse cryptocurrencies. Sure, a cash underworld economy will stick around, but it will become the exception.

## Financial Standards and Infrastructure

### The Role of Standards

Every major technology needs rules and standards to work smoothly. Just like internet protocols like HTTP and TCP/IP became the standard for web communication, the future of finance will run on standardized blockchain protocols. Understanding which projects are building toward the future can help you position yourself wisely. Large banks, institutions, and asset managers will follow strict international standards to ensure they can safely and efficiently adopt blockchain technology.

Why standards matter:

- Interoperability: They let different blockchains, banks, and applications "speak the same language," enabling cross-border payments and multi-asset settlements.

- Trust and Security: Adhering to industry standards like ISO 27001 and SOC 2 assures robust data protection, compliance, and customer trust.

- Scalability and Efficiency: Standards reduce fragmentation, lower integration costs, and allow rapid innovation at scale.

Key examples driving the new financial system:

- ISO 20022 – Global financial messaging standard. This enables crypto platforms to "talk" to traditional banks and payment systems in a consistent and structured way.

- ISO/TR 23455 – Defines standards for smart contracts, helping developers create secure, consistent digital agreements. Think of it like grammar rules. If everyone follows them, communication is smooth and safe.

- ISO 22739 – Defines blockchain terminology for consistent adoption across countries and institutions. This ensures that core terms like "wallet" mean the same thing in the U.S., Europe, Asia, etc.

- SOC 2 - A security framework that specifies how organizations should protect customer data from unauthorized access, security incidents, and other vulnerabilities. The American Institute of Certified Public Accountants (AICPA) developed SOC 2 around five Trust Services Criteria: security, availability, processing integrity, confidentiality, and privacy.

- ISO 27001 – A globally recognized information security standard. It specifies the requirements for establishing, implementing, maintaining, and continually improving an information security management system (ISMS). If a crypto follows ISO 27001, it means they are treating security and compliance with professional care.

These standards form the foundation for how traditional finance and blockchain systems will integrate, enabling regulatory compliance, global interoperability, and long-term trust in digital assets.

Once these frameworks are in place, institutions can begin building real applications that connect existing financial infrastructure with blockchain networks.

Several organizations are already applying these principles in practical ways, from supply chain tracking to cross-border banking and global trade finance.

**Case Studies**

The following examples show how blockchain is already being used in real-world systems. These projects demonstrate how established standards and enterprise frameworks allow blockchain to integrate with industries like supply chains, banking, and international trade.

- **IBM Food Trust**
  Uses Hyperledger Fabric and follows enterprise data-security standards such as **ISO 27001**, enabling secure supply-chain transparency.

- **VeChain**
  Integrates with supply-chain systems and enterprise data standards to track product authenticity and provenance.

- **PM Coin (JPMorgan)**
  Built to integrate with ISO 20022 messaging standards used by global banking networks.

- **BIS mBridge**
  Designed for central bank digital currency interoperability, aligning with international financial messaging standards such as ISO 20022.

- **ITFA**
  Works on digital trade finance standards and tokenized documentation frameworks that align with global financial

messaging systems.

As blockchain systems move from experimentation into real economic infrastructure, governments and regulators have begun stepping in to define the rules that will govern this new financial landscape.

## Regulation

### New Crypto Regulations

What is notable about these bills is that they were passed with bipartisan support, which is rare in today's divided political environment. This shows both sides recognize the financial opportunity this new system represents. But none of this operates in isolation.

DeFi, blockchains, and always-on financial systems feel abstract-intellectual, digital, weightless. In reality, they are anchored to something very physical. Every transaction, every smart contract, every AI-driven decision ultimately runs on electricity. Energy exposes a truth that markets alone can't ignore. Scale changes everything.

When financial systems begin to consume power at the scale of cities, governments stop viewing them as niche technologies and start treating them as critical infrastructure. This is the point where innovation collides with policy.

Regulation isn't arriving because blockchain failed. It's arriving because blockchain is succeeding- visibly, rapidly, and at too large a scale to ignore.

One of the most immediate areas regulators are focusing on is taxation. As cryptocurrency adoption grows, governments are working to determine how digital assets should be reported, taxed, and integrated into existing financial systems.

## Tax and Policy

### Broker Reporting Requirements

Starting in 2026, crypto exchanges will be required to file the new IRS Form 1099-DA for digital asset sales. While this move is intended to close the multibillion-dollar "crypto tax gap," platforms like Coinbase warned that the IRS may be overwhelmed by the massive influx of data.

### Staking and Mining Rewards

Some witnesses suggested taxing staking and mining rewards only when they are sold, not when they are generated. Supporters said this approach would align crypto taxation with traditional assets and prevent double taxation. Opponents argued it could allow indefinite tax deferral and reduce revenue collection.

### Small Transaction Relief

Proposals to exempt everyday crypto transactions under $300 from capital gains reporting gained traction. Proponents argue this would simplify compliance and promote broader adoption of crypto for daily use, while critics warned it could create tax loopholes and lead to billions in lost revenue.

### Crypto Taxes in the Senate

On October 1, 2025, the U.S. Senate held a hearing on how to tax cryptocurrency. Lawmakers debated whether small, everyday crypto transactions, such as buying coffee, should be tax-free, whether staking and mining rewards should be taxed only when sold, and how new IRS reporting rules will affect exchanges and investors. Supporters of looser rules argued that they would make crypto easier to use in everyday life, while critics warned that such changes could create tax loopholes. The hearing highlighted Congress's growing interest in clearer tax rules but also revealed uncertainty over how to balance innovation with tax compliance.

**IRS Guidance Updates**: Recent IRS notices clarified that unrealized crypto gains are excluded from the corporate minimum tax, providing more explicit guidance for companies holding digital assets. Still, the broader debate revealed a tension between fostering innovation and ensuring tax compliance.

While governments are still working to define the regulatory framework around digital assets, individuals and businesses are already navigating this evolving system in real time. Understanding how to operate within this new financial landscape is becoming an increasingly valuable skill.

### Navigating the Shift

The challenge many people will face is learning how to operate and navigate blockchain technology.

Think of the people who once said:

*"Why would I need to send an email?".*

*Or "Why get the news online when a newspaper costs 35 cents?"*

We are moving from the dial-up version of money to fiber-optic speed:

Instant, borderless, and always on.

Companies that do not integrate these new technologies will face some of the same consequences as other companies that resisted new technology in the past. A good example of this is Blockbuster. There is only one still standing today (2025) because it did not evolve to streaming.

### Focus Areas & Financial Mindset for the New Economy

As of now, your attention should be on the following key sectors:

**Real World Assets (RWAs):** RWAs convert traditional assets like U.S. Treasuries, stocks, real estate, and commodities into digital tokens you can trade. Institutions like BlackRock and JPMorgan are leading the adoption. The benefits of this are:

- Fractional ownership - Buy a small piece of a house or treasury bond
- Trade 24/7 - No more waiting for bank hours
- More liquidity – Easier buying and selling
- Bridges traditional finance (TradFi) and crypto (DeFi): Combining traditional finance with decentralized systems.

**Layer 1 Blockchain Projects**: These are the operating systems of the blockchain world. Examples: Ethereum, Solana, XRPL, Hyperledger, etc. They are powering everything from finance to gaming to supply chain. They are the infrastructure of Web3.

**Artificial Intelligence (AI):** AI + Blockchain

AI is being used for fraud detection, risk scoring, and smart contract auditing. AI bots monitor the crypto markets 24/7, executing trades in DeFi. This convergence drives new opportunities for programmable economies. Ex. food ordering, hotel bookings, flights, car services, etc.

**Decentralized Finance (DeFi):** Possibilities, Not Hype

DeFi is unlocking the future by replacing traditional intermediaries with smart contracts for open, efficient financial services. Its core applications include:

- Peer-to-peer lending and borrowing (e.g., Aave)
- Decentralized exchanges to trade crypto instantly (e.g., Uniswap)

- Earning interest with yield farming and staking
- Promote financial inclusion for the unbanked with just a smartphone
- Insure your assets

Looking ahead, DeFi is growing even more with regulatory progress, stronger security, sustainability efforts, and deeper Web3 integration. In 2025, DeFi's TVL, the total amount of crypto currently deposited into DeFi platforms, has now exceeded $156 billion, and growth is expected to continue.

However, DeFi is not without risks, such as:

- Bugs in the smart contract
- Network congestion is causing slow speeds
- Environmental concerns

Developers are working hard to make ongoing improvements and address these issues.

Overall, DeFi empowers global economies by giving more people access to financial tools, fostering innovation, and bridging traditional and decentralized finance.

**Early Action = Long-Term Advantage**

Most everyday investors, commonly referred to as retail investors, tend to enter the market only after cryptocurrency makes mainstream headlines. But by then, it is often too late to make a significant impact. Prices will already have surged, making early entry critical. The best gains usually go to early movers who research and invest before the hype.

In this new financial system, you are the bank.

With crypto and DeFi, you can:

- Lend your assets to earn interest
- Borrow against your crypto
- Earn a passive income called yield
- Buy and sell assets
- Participate in financial systems once reserved for the elite or big institutions
- Create instant liquidity by turning RWA into NFTs

The longer you delay understanding this system, the more likely you are to be left behind.

If you are fortunate enough to have liquidity on the sidelines, now is the time to protect and elevate your financial position. Crypto is not just about trading; it is a new economic structure, one that rewards early adopters who take the time to learn, adapt, and position themselves strategically.

At this point, a pattern should be emerging.

Money is becoming programmable. Infrastructure is becoming digital. Energy is becoming strategic. Regulation is chasing reality. Intelligence, both human and artificial, is being forced to adapt.

These are not separate trends. They are pieces of the same transition. Understanding how they connect is the difference between reacting to the future and positioning yourself ahead of it.

### The Opportunity Ahead

You have an opportunity to be part of one of the most significant transitions in financial history. Never before has the movement of money and value changed so rapidly or at such a global scale. This is not just about profits; it's about being present as new financial systems, technologies, and opportunities emerge.

Consider Sophie, a novice investor who discovered a DeFi yield strategy by chance. By investing a small amount, she experienced firsthand how decentralized finance can provide steady growth and open doors previously reserved for institutions. Her story reflects a broader reality: individuals can now participate in and shape the future of finance in ways that were unimaginable just a decade ago.

Think about it:

- When Disney became a publicly traded company, did your parents invest?
- When Microsoft rose to dominance, did they invest?
- When Amazon started in the 1990s, did they invest?

Most people did not. And it was not because they did not want to, but because they did not know how to. These companies became juggernauts, and early investors saw life-changing returns. By 2030, we will see a similar transformation in how we purchase, sell, trade, invest, loan, borrow, and fund money. Everything about money is changing, and you still have time to be a part of it.

**The Next Bull Market & Why Timing Matters**

Timing plays a decisive role in the crypto market. Periods of rapid expansion, commonly referred to as bull markets, have historically created the greatest opportunities for wealth generation. But they also expose a simple reality: most participants enter too late and exit too early.

Many observers have pointed to a four-year cycle, where markets move from explosive highs to deep corrections, often falling 70–80% before recovering. Within these cycles, capital has historically flowed in stages: first into Bitcoin, then Ethereum, followed by large-cap altcoins, and eventually into smaller, more speculative assets.

However, this framework has not always held. Recent market behavior suggests a deeper driver beneath these patterns.

Market analyst Raoul Pal argues that crypto cycles are more closely tied to global liquidity. When money supply expands and financial conditions loosen, risk assets including crypto, tend to rise. When liquidity contracts, markets tighten, and crypto often experiences the most severe drawdowns.

This shifts the focus from fixed cycles to macro conditions. Rather than asking where we are in a predefined timeline, the more important question becomes: where are we in the global liquidity cycle?

Understanding this distinction can help investors move beyond simple narratives and better position themselves for the next phase of the market.

When the tide of money turns up, investors feel safer and take more risks.

When it turns down, they get cautious and pull back.

BTC and ETH tend to rise rapidly when the market is bullish and conditions are favorable. The four-year rhythm is not just "magic." These price surges usually happen when two things line up:

- Liquidity wave - A wave of new money entering markets
- Narrative wave - A wave of big news or events, such as BTC halving, new technologies, or more buyers

However, this cycle is already taking a different form.

In previous years, the market was primarily driven by crypto enthusiasts, retail traders, and tech insiders. Now, we are seeing unprecedented levels of mainstream adoption, including:

- Hedge funds
- Large institutional investors
- Corporations

- Central banks
- U.S. states
- Entire countries

This shift changes everything.

- **ISO 20022**, the new global financial messaging standard, goes live in November 2025, streamlining international money movement. It standardizes payment data, making it easier for banks and crypto systems to interoperate.
- **401(k) plans** will include crypto investment options, following a recent executive order signed by Donald Trump.
- **Digital Commodity Consumer Protection Act** (DCCPA) focuses on oversight for buying and selling crypto commodities like Bitcoin and Ethereum. It requires crypto exchanges to follow stricter customer protection rules. This will strengthen consumer safeguards but could raise some concerns over Commodity Futures Trading Commission (CFTC)-SEC overlap.

When the Federal Reserve cuts interest rates, lending expands, and liquidity returns, especially to risk-on assets like crypto. On September 18, 2025, the Fed cut rates slightly by 25 basis points (0.25%), lighting the fuse and boosting investor confidence. This led to increased flows into crypto ETFs. Historically, September is rough for crypto, with average losses around 6-7%. But 2025 is different. We are looking at an 8% gain so far, with prices swinging from a low of $107,000 on September 1st to highs near $118,000 mid-month. That makes it the best September performance since 2012. While October leads to a massive letdown for 2025.

## Financial System Risk

### It Ain't All Sweet

Following the explosive highs of mid-2025, the cryptocurrency market entered one of the toughest corrections in recent memory. What began as a healthy pullback turned into a full-on bear phase as global uncertainty renewed. The government shutdown, 100% U.S.–China tariff threats, and anxious investors all collided. Liquidity dried up, trading volume thinned, and what was meant to be a brief breather became a deep test of conviction for everyone in the space.

The exhaustion was thick. Exchanges were quiet. Even the most bullish traders started asking the dreaded question: “Is this another crypto wall?”

The energy felt different this time, not just because prices had fallen, but because confidence had cracked. The institutional “smart money” that had flowed in through Bitcoin ETFs and other regulated products earlier in the year was now quietly taking profits and stepping to the sidelines. Ironically, crypto initially handled the first round of tariff announcements earlier in the year with surprising strength, rallying as investors viewed it as a hedge against political and regulatory instability. But the shutdown has shifted that narrative. Until this catalyst is lifted and confidence in U.S. financial policy returns, the market recovery will remain capped.

### System Failure?

Then came the event nobody saw coming.

Within hours of the surprise tariff announcement, nearly every major centralized exchange went dark. The failure was instant and systemic:

Trading engines froze.

Wallets lagged.

Stop losses failed to trigger.

The market tanked faster than anyone could react. In a few terrifying minutes, some assets had zero bids at all. Bitcoin dropped nearly 16%, while altcoins collapsed 60 to 80% on average.

In less than a day, over $20 billion in leveraged positions were wiped out, though many analysts believe the actual figure was far higher.

What made it worse wasn't just the price action; it was the total breakdown of trust. Users logged in to see their position balances zeroed. While exchanges issued only vague statements about "technical issues." Binance, Coinbase, and others were overwhelmed. For many, it felt like an instant replay of the FTX collapse, only this time, the losses were system-wide and irreversible in real time.

**The Mystery of the $150 Million Ghost**

As the dust settled, one discovery added a conspiracy layer of intrigue.

The day before the crash, an anonymous wallet, newly created with no prior history, opened a $50 million hyper-leveraged short on Bitcoin futures through a smaller derivatives platform. The trade was executed using a decentralized protocol like Hyperliquid, where users can access perpetual futures with extreme leverage (often 25x–100x), a more advanced form of trading.

When prices collapsed, that position skyrocketed to roughly $150 million in profit before being routed through mixing services and disappearing from traceable view.

Investigators verified the trade data but could not identify the owner. Some called it perfect timing; others suspected it may have been the precise shove that accelerated the downward spiral.

The tariff headlines dominated mainstream media, overshadowing the exchange outages and market irregularities. Inside the crypto community, though, the question lingered: Was this simply macro pressure or something deeper in the code, perhaps even deliberate?

### The Perfect Storm

Post-crash investigations eventually revealed the technical spark that turned panic into catastrophe.

A stablecoin, USDe, de-pegged on Binance, falling from $1.00 to $0.65 after a bad price feed misinformed the exchange's core trading systems.

That single misfire had cascading consequences:

- **Automatic Liquidations:** Accounts using USDe as collateral were instantly flagged as under-collateralized, triggering forced sell-offs.

- **The Chain Reaction:** Automated systems continued dumping into an already broken market. Without circuit breaker safeguards common in traditional finance, the fall fed on itself.

When the dust cleared, more than $1.6 million trading accounts were liquidated within 24 hours, erasing nearly half a trillion dollars in total market value. Exchanges issued apologies and promised reforms. Binance launched a compensation review, conceding its systems couldn't keep up.

### The Old Truth Relearned

For shaken investors, the damage was done. Confidence in centralized exchanges fell, accelerating the migration toward self-custody and decentralized platforms.

Ironically, the crash accomplished what years of education and outreach could not: it reminded everyone of the oldest truth in crypto:

"Not your keys, not your coins."

Those hit hardest were the futures and leverage traders. If you weren't borrowing or if your exposure stayed below roughly 30% of your collateral, you likely weathered the storm. For everyone else, October 10, 2025 became a brutal reminder that leverage magnifies both opportunity and destruction at lightning speed.

**Lessons Learned**

The October 2025 crash exposed the weaknesses that had been hiding beneath all the progress: poor risk management, over-reliance on single data sources, and centralized control points that could fail simultaneously. It also forced the entire ecosystem, from stablecoin issuers to regulators, to confront the extent to which crypto had become interconnected.

And yet, as it always does, the market kept going. Prices recovered slowly, but trust will take longer to rebuild. What matters most is what comes next. Every crash, every correction, every painful liquidation writes another lesson into the blockchain's story of resilience.

Crypto doesn't die, it evolves. The October crash wasn't the end. It was a brutal reminder that the road to a decentralized financial world isn't smooth, but it's still being paved, block by block.

**The Government Shutdown Catalyst**

As of early November 2025, the United States has once again entered a record-tying government shutdown. A stark reminder of political gridlock at a time when global markets are already under heavy strain. This shutdown, stretching beyond previous records, has effectively frozen key economic operations: federal contracts are paused, data releases delayed.

While the broader stock market has managed to stay afloat, risk-on sectors like technology and digital assets are feeling the pressure. The uncertainty is pushing investors toward defensive positions and cash, reducing liquidity in crypto markets just weeks after the October 10th system failure. Traders are calling it the "perfect storm" with the shutdown, tariff scares, and lingering exchange outages all combining to test reaction across every market.

In a sense, the government standoff has become symbolic of the broader problem: systems built for the last century are colliding with the realities of the new one. The crypto market doesn't just need better code or cleaner regulations; it needs stability in the legacy systems it aims to complement, not replace.

**A Glimpse of Light Ahead**

Since Bitcoin's all-time high in October, something important has happened and most people missed it.

For the first time in a long while, Bitcoin stopped being the center of the market.

While BTC moved sideways in consolidation, money did not leave the system. It rotated elsewhere. Traditional markets quietly outperformed crypto. The S&P 500 pushed higher, equities held strength, and gold and silver surged into year-end, outperforming not only Bitcoin, but most altcoins as well.

That rotation matters.

It tells us this wasn't simply a "crypto bear market" it was a risk reallocation. When uncertainty rose, capital didn't disappear; it moved. Investors sought assets with clearer cash flows, long-standing trust, and lower volatility. Gold and silver reclaimed their role as safe havens, while equities absorbed liquidity many expected to flow into crypto.

Crypto didn't lose relevance, it lost priority. And that distinction is critical. 2025 was supposed to be *the* bull market. Instead, it became something else entirely:
a sorting year.

Liquidity didn't flood every risk asset equally. It became selective. Bitcoin stalled. Altcoins struggled. Meanwhile, metals closed the year strong, and traditional markets reminded everyone that capital seeks stability before speculation.

The old playbook - buy anything, wait, and hope - stopped working.

Meme coins collapsed first. Low-effort Layer 2s followed. Projects without real users, real revenue, or real progress faded away quietly. When Solana took a major hit earlier in 2025, it wiped out an entire class of speculative excess. At the time, it felt destructive. In hindsight, it was necessary.

That purge didn't weaken the market, it cleared it.

This is how new cycles are built: not through endless expansion, but through pressure, discipline, and survival.

And that discipline is exactly what sets the stage for the future.

The crypto market today is no longer just a retail-driven market. Institutions, asset managers, energy companies, AI firms, and real-world asset issuers are now active participants. These players don't chase hype. They demand reliability, compliance, execution, and real-world utility.

That changes the rules.

As we move into 2026, many Layer 2s and even some Layer 1s will face an uncomfortable reality: deliver real value, or disappear.

Projects that fail to show progress, development activity, or real-world integration won't collapse dramatically. They'll simply be ignored. Meanwhile, platforms that continue to build, scale, and integrate into broader financial and industrial systems will move forward, even without hype.

This is no longer a game of price alone.

It's a game of infrastructure, endurance, and relevance.

That's why the next bull cycle won't look like the last one. It won't be a single explosive move led only by Bitcoin and blindly followed by everything else. It will be uneven, sector-driven, more strategic-and far less forgiving.

But that's not bad news.

Opportunity doesn't appear when capital is euphoric.

It appears when capital has already tested every alternative; stocks, metals, cash and begins rotating back toward growth with clearer rules and stronger foundations.

2025 was the reset.

2026 is the rebuild.

Crypto didn't fail. It matured.

And the projects that survive this phase will shape the next decade.

**Date Event Description / Context**

- January 2025: Crypto market review (Post-2024 consolidation) Market stabilizes after late-2024 volatility. Institutional positioning and ETF inflows build momentum.

- April 05, 2025: Stablecoin market $238B (mainstream adoption milestone). Stablecoins like USDC and USDT see record circulation due to integrations with Visa and PayPal.

- April 09, 2025: U.S. raises tariffs on China to 125%. Start of trade tensions — global markets show resilience; crypto remains stable as investors view it as a hedge.

- May 7, 2025: Continued infrastructure improvements across the ecosystem .Overall, Efforts focus on better usability, efficiency, and preparation for future scalability.

- May 12, 2025: U.S.–China trade truce (tariffs cut to ~30%). Temporary easing of trade war pressures; markets stabilize briefly as macro risk cools.

- June 15, 2025: DeFi staking growth (EigenLayer TVL > $11B). Liquid staking surges; Protocols innovate with real yield and institutional-grade security.

- July 13-17, 2025: GENIUS Conference: Web3, AI, and blockchain convergence; Global summit emphasizes AI-crypto integration; Investor optimism peaks mid-year.

- August 21-23, 2025: Jackson Hole Symposium Federal Reserve (Fed) policy discussions signal possible rate cuts later in the year;

Markets turn cautiously bullish.

- September 17, 2025: Potential first Fed rate cut (if inflation stays low); Anticipation builds for monetary easing – stage for a year-end rally narrative.
- Early October 2025: Record-tying U.S. Government shutdown begins; Federal operations halt; Markets lose confidence; Pressure added to an already weak crypto sentiment.
- October 10, 2025: System failure & crypto market crash; Centralized exchanges freeze; $20B+ liquidated. Confidence collapses further; Migration to self-custody surges.
- November 15, 2025: Stablecoin legislation progresses (House/Senate reconciliation); Clarity Act and stablecoin framework near approval; Restores cautious optimism.
- December 03, 2025: Ethereum "Fusaka" upgrade Major network scalability and security enhancement. Lays groundwork for mass adoption and lower gas fees.
- December 12, 2025: Federal Reserve rate cute and Bitcoin Reserve Act hearings; Rate cuts renew liquidity flow; Bitcoin and DeFi lead year-end rally into 2026.

# Opportunity and Strategy

### The Next Wave of Wealth Creation

We are entering a new era of wealth creation. Some believe the world's first trillionaire could emerge from the crypto and blockchain space.

In past economic crises like the 1980 recession or the 2008 financial crisis, people were almost entirely dependent on traditional financial systems. Savings, payments, credit, and access to capital all flowed through centralized institutions. If those systems slowed or failed, there were few alternatives.

That is beginning to change.

Today, a parallel financial system is emerging, one that gives individuals more direct control over how they store, move, and access value.

In parts of the world facing economic pressure or sanctions, these digital rails are already being used as alternatives. Iran has leveraged energy resources to support Bitcoin mining and crypto-based transactions. Venezuela has increasingly turned to stablecoins like USDT in sectors tied to its oil economy.

These are not theoretical use cases, They are early signals of how financial systems adapt under constraint.

When traditional systems tighten, new ones don't ask for permission; they route around them.

Here is how crypto and blockchain technology are changing the financial game:

- No intermediaries – You control your money, not the bank.
- Instant, 24/7 transactions – Send or receive your money anytime, no banking hours or transfer delays.
- Low-cost global payments – Send money across borders quickly and cheaply.
- Access for the unbanked – Billions without bank accounts can now participate in the global economy using just a smartphone.
- Enhanced privacy and security – Your data and funds are yours, not held by a company or bank.
- Programmable money – Tools like smart contracts allow for automated payments, loans, and financial services.

Traditional banks can control access to your money, freeze your accounts, and limit withdrawals or delays. They also remain vulnerable to systemic failures. With blockchain technology, the rules change. You can own your assets, control your financial destiny, and reduce dependence on centralized institutions. In the crypto community, there is a well-known saying, "Not your keys, not your wallet." This means that if you do not control the private keys, you do not truly control the money. You hold a claim or receipt, not the asset. Use an exchange to buy and sell. Use a self-custody wallet to safely keep your assets and ensure they are truly yours. Financial freedom is being redefined, and cryptocurrency is leading the way.

**Clever Positioning in the Crypto Market**

Positioning yourself wisely in the crypto market requires more than chasing hype; it demands education, discipline, and a clear strategy in light of rapidly evolving trends. The following improvements provide more precise flow, actionable formatting, and highlight where credible citations can enhance the section:

Right now, we are in a moment where those who have been paying attention to the crypto market, gathering accurate information, and making wise investment choices (not just gambling) have already created generational wealth. Just as the beginning of the internet in the 1990s transformed how we communicate and access information, or how the introduction of credit cards revolutionized consumer spending in the mid-20th century, cryptocurrencies are set to redefine the landscape of finance and investment. The parallels are clear: early adopters of groundbreaking technologies often reap significant rewards, and the crypto space is no different. Much like those who recognized the potential of digital communication or electronic payments, today's informed crypto investors are positioned to capitalize on the next significant financial evolution.

While some have profited by speculating on meme coins or chasing market trends, clever positioning means understanding what you're investing in, the underlying technology, its purpose, and its long-term value.

Think of it like the dot-com era. The internet created tremendous opportunities, but also heavy losses for those who treated it as a gold rush or a get-rich-quick scheme. They acted on fear of missing out (FOMO) instead of research and bought whatever was trending. Chasing prices because "someone said to buy it" is different from building smart, well-researched positions in assets you genuinely understand and believe in. And yes, a lot of people went broke as well. But that's a part of the investment game, especially when you do not do your best to minimize risk.

This brings us to the next layer of the story.

When macro conditions tighten, interest rates rise, liquidity dries up, and trust in institutions weakens, people don't just complain. They look for alternatives. Historically, those alternatives were limited. Today, they are not.

This is where DeFi stops being an experiment and starts acting as a pressure valve. It doesn't exist in a vacuum. It exists because the traditional financial system creates friction, delay, and barriers precisely when people need speed, access, and control the most.

That said....

As the saying goes, "*Scared money don't make no money.*"

To position yourself strategically in the crypto market:

- Define Your Why: Know your purpose for investing in crypto. Are you in it for long-term growth, passive income, or ecosystem participation?

- Research Assets Thoroughly: Investigate what each asset does and understand the problem it is solving.

- Risk Management: Never invest more than you are willing to lose. Prioritize risk management over chasing high returns.

- Stay Informed: Regularly update your knowledge about market trends and new technologies. Refer back to this checklist as you make decisions.

**Where to Begin? Follow Your Interests**

Not sure which crypto to research? Start with what interests you. Pick a topic or industry you care about, find real-world use cases that align with your goals, and learn how it fits into the big picture. If you are familiar with trading stocks or long-term investing, apply the same principles here: study fundamentals, identify trends, and focus on utility. For those who want a lower-risk entry point into crypto, stablecoins offer a great starting lane. These are digital tokens like USDC and USDT that are pegged 1:1 to the U.S. dollar. They offer price stability and can earn DeFi yields (interest) when used in lending or staking protocols, making them a smart tool for conservative growth without direct exposure to volatile assets.

And now, there's an even simpler approach: yield-bearing stablecoins. These are next generation stablecoins that generate passive yield automatically, just by holding them. Think of them like blockchain-native savings accounts, the value stays pegged to the dollar, but your balance slowly grows. No trading, no staking, no farming required.

On Solana, the stablecoin sUSD (by Solayer) is backed by short-term U.S. Treasuries and offers yields. On Sui, the upcoming USDsui delivers yield directly to holders as a form of built-in income. These coins provide a safe, beginner-friendly way to explore DeFi and understand how APRs, staking, and on-chain protocols work, without needing to read complex charts or time the market.

It's hands-on experience with the financial layer of crypto, for savers, not just speculators.

My focus has been on the banking and financial sector. Here are some of the leading finance-focused cryptos to research:

- Ripple (XRP)
- Solana (SOL)
- Ethereum (ETH)
- Avalanche (AVAX)
- Hedera (HBAR)
- Stronghold (SHX)
- Stellar (XLM)
- Chainlink (Link)

- XDC Network (XDC)
- Tron (TRX)
- Crypto.com (CRO)
- Iota network (IOTA)
- Polkadot (DOT)
- QUANT Network (QNT)
- Algorand (ALGO)

And more!

| Blockchain/ Network | Consensus Mechanism | Main Use Case | Native Token | Transaction Speed (TPS) | Unique Features |
|---|---|---|---|---|---|
| Bitcoin (BTC) | Proof of Work (PoW) | Store of value, peer-to-peer payments | BTC | Payments BTC7 | First cryptocurrency; decentralized; limited supply (21M); often called "digital gold"; mining requires specialized hardware. |
| Ripple (XRP) | Ripple Protocol Consensus Algorithm (RPCA) | Cross-border payments, liquidity for financial institutions | XRP | 1,500+ | Designed for banks, pre-mined supply, ISO 20022 compliant, focuses on fast, cheap international transfers, not entirely decentralized. |
| Stellar (XLM) | Stellar Consensus Protocol (SCP) / Federated Byzantine Agreement | Cross-border payments, financial inclusion for the unbanked | XLM | 1,000+ | Non-profit oriented; integrates with banks for multi-currency transactions; anti-spam fees; ISO 20022 compliant; focuses on accessibility. |
| Solana (SOL) | Proof of History (PoH) + Proof of Stake (PoS | High-speed dApps, DeFi, NFTs | SOL | Up to 65,000 (theoretical), 2,000 practical | Extremely fast and low-cost; history of network outages; focuses on scalability without sharding; used for gaming and high-throughput apps. |
| Hedera (HBAR) | Asynchronous Byzantine Fault Tolerance (aBFT) | Enterprise applications, DeFi, NFTs | HBAR | 10,000+ (certified) | Governed by a council of global enterprises, ISO 20022 compliant, high security, and fairness, not fully permissionless. |
| Axelar (AXL) | Delegated proof of stake (DPOS) using Tendermint BFT | Enables secure cross-chain communication, token transfers, and multichain dApp integration | AXL | Up to 10,000 TPS (depends on connected chains) | General Message passing (GMP), gas fee abstraction, universal API for developers, secure validator-based bridging, and support for 50+ blockchains. |
| Stronghold (SHX) | Proof-of-Agreement (PoA) | Payments, DeFi, merchant rewards, and financing | SHX | Same as Stellar (1,000+) | Built on Stellar for climate-friendly transactions; fixed supply (100B); used for real-time settlements, fee discounts, and governance; also available as ERC-20 on Ethereum; no ICO. |
| Chainlink (LINK) | Reputation-based with staking (not a consensus for blockchain) | Providing real-world data to smart contracts | LINK | Varies by host chain | Not a standalone blockchain; bridges off-chain data to on-chain; essential for DeFi; supports multiple chains; uses ECDSA/secp256k1 and EdDSA/curve25519. |
| XDC Network (XDC) | Delegated Proof of Stake (DPoS) using Tendermint BFT | Trade finance, global payments | XDC | 2,000+ | ISO 20022 compliant; enterprise-focused; supports smart contracts; bridges traditional finance and blockchain. |
| Tron (TRX) | Delegated Proof of Stake (DPoS) using Tendermint BFT | dApps, content sharing, DeFi | TRX | 2,000+ | Acquired BitTorrent; focuses on entertainment and digital content; high throughput; transitioned to a DeFi platform. |
| Crypto.com / Cronos (CRO) | Tendermint (Proof of Stake variant | Payments, DeFi, NFTs, exchange ecosystem | CRO | High (thousands) | Tied to the Crypto.com platform, supports Visa cards and staking, bridges to the Cosmos ecosystem, and focuses on user adoption through rewards. |
| Quant (QNT) | N/A (API gateway for multi-DLT) | Connecting blockchains for enterprise | QNT | Varies by connected chains | Not a blockchain; enables multi-chain apps; ISO 20022 compliant; focuses on interoperability between legacy systems and DLTs. |
| Polkadot (DOT) | Nominated Proof of Stake (NPoS) | Blockchain interoperability, parachains for specialized apps | DOT | Varies (scalable with parachains, up to thousands) | Enables cross-chain communication, parachain auctions, and is founded by an Ethereum co-founder, supporting multiple signing algorithms. |

*Cryptocurrency Table (as of 2025) An institutional crypto market survey published by Sygnum Bank (a Swiss-based digital asset bank). The report, released in 2023, surveyed professional investors and aligns closely with the statistics.*

Research suggests that tokenized RWAs have seen substantial growth, with total value locked (TVL) rising from approximately $6.3 billion in late 2023 to around $15-24 billion by mid-to-late 2025. This represents a 2.5x to 4x growth, showing increasing trust and interest.

We are already seeing early signs of what may come next. Not long ago, XRP was trading between $0.35 and $0.50. Today, it trades dramatically higher. And XRP is not alone. Across the crypto market, many digital assets have experienced significant growth as adoption continues to accelerate.

**The Future Leaders**

As the crypto ecosystem matures, the next generation of industry leaders is beginning to take shape. In this new financial era, the next Google, Amazon, or Tesla could emerge from a blockchain project.

While many focus on Bitcoin (BTC), the real disruptors will be next-generation blockchains (altcoins) with practical use cases and projects designed to transform industries through real-world applications and utility, such as:

- Finance
- Real estate
- Healthcare
- Gaming
- Supply chains
- Energy
- Communication
- Infrastructure

**Your Move**

The next era of money is not just something you read about; it's a choice you make. You don't have to be an expert or a risk-taker to start; what matters most is informed, consistent action. Missing out on the early internet or tech booms taught many people the value of curiosity and the willingness to learn. Now, the same kind of opportunity is emerging as finance becomes digital, decentralized, and accessible to all.

The next era of money is not a theory; it is a choice. I am not here to convince anyone. I know what it is like to miss out because I did not understand something early enough. I remember when my sister told me about GameStop *before* the hype. My response to her was, "Oni, nobody even buys games from GameStop anymore." If I could use that slap-your-forehead emoji right now, I would. So, when she told me about crypto, I listened. That moment took me from stock trading to reading whitepapers and roadmaps instead of balance sheets: same game, different language. The FUD never left. But I stayed curious.

One thing has not changed: Almost everyone wants to know how to create extra income!

Here's your first challenge to take action: This week, choose one cryptocurrency that interests you, research its fundamentals, and open a demo account on a trading platform to get hands-on with market simulations. To help you get started, I recommend trying out beginner-friendly platforms like Coinbase and Binance, as they offer easy-to-navigate interfaces and a variety of educational resources. This small step can transform passive learning into active engagement, setting the foundation for deeper exploration in the exciting world of digital assets. There's no better time to jump in and see where this new financial frontier can take you.

We went from letters to email, from dial-up to streaming. Now, we are shifting from slow-moving banks to instant, borderless value. Money that moves like a message: fast, simple, and global. You can sit on the sidelines and watch it happen, or you can step into it.

People often think of crypto as a "degenerate stock market." It is not. You are not investing in companies; you are buying slices of the internet. It's digital real estate. Let's take XRP, for example. In 2021, the SEC sued Ripple (XRP)over whether XRP's institutional sales were "investment contracts." This suit caused XRP to be delisted from many U.S. exchanges, and the price plummeted. During this case, the court distinguished between two types of sales. They are:

- Institutional sales - sold directly to hedge funds and companies (deemed securities).

- Programmatic sales - sold to the public on crypto exchanges with no direct contact between Ripple and the buyer (not deemed securities).

By August 2025, the SEC officially ended its lawsuit against Ripple. The agency confirmed the closure, with Ripple agreeing to pay the $125 million fine without further appeals from either side. The fine was related only to Ripple's unregistered institutional sales of XRP. It was not for XRP sold to the public on exchanges. Those were considered programmatic sales and were not securities. No fraud was alleged. Additionally, Ripple's "bad actor" disqualification was waived, allowing the company to continue operating normally. The court finalized this on August 23, 2025, marking the end of the multi-year saga. The case ultimately boosted the legitimacy, of not only Ripple, but the entire crypto industry. It marked a turning point toward absolute legal clarity and a meaningful distinction between crypto tokens and traditional securities.

The tech giants are already making moves. Google and Meta have partnered with Sui to bring blockchain tools and data to developers. Coinbase Ventures is backing SocialFi and more. Fortune 500 companies are investing in building and adopting cryptocurrency infrastructure.

McLaren racing joined the Hedera council. That kind of move says blockchain is not a trend; it is becoming the next layer of the internet.

Interest is heating up across the space. Bitcoin is the Michael Jordan as the icon. Then Ethereum is LeBron, the MVP of infrastructure. And Solana? That is Steph Curry, a flashy, fast player who is redefining the game. Others are finding their lanes as adoption grows.

Every major shift looks obvious in hindsight. Disney, Microsoft, and Amazon... early investors were rewarded. The winners were not always the loudest. They were early, informed, and consistent. Crypto is that kind of turning point. It is not just hype or memes. It is a fundamental tool for solving real problems. Yes, prices swing. But in those swings, fortunes are made, industries are disrupted, and value is redefined. And as liquidity and TVL increase, volatility will decrease. The institutions are already her e.

This isn't about gambling. It is about learning the basics and using them with discipline. If you can send an email, you can send value. If you can protect a password, you can protect a wallet. If you can build a savings habit, you can build a crypto plan and stick to it. Here is the simple playbook to get in the arena calmly, intelligently, on your terms:

- **Educate**: Pick a few trusted sources and study the basic wallets, keys, networks, fees, and security.

- **Secure**: Set up a reputable wallet, enable 2FA, and write down your recovery phrase offline.

- **Start Small**: Dollar-cost average an amount that you're comfortable with. Consistency beats intensity. There is also the stablecoin strategy that I mentioned earlier in the book.

- **Focus**: Keep a core in high-conviction assets; research select projects with real-world utility.

- **Protect**: Diversify across custody, keep records, understand taxes, and your local regulations.

- **Plan**: Set time horizons and rules before you buy. Automate contributions where possible. Review quarterly.

You do not need to predict the following headline. You need a system you can stick to, especially when headlines change. That is how wealth is built - quietly, methodically, and over time.

The window is open. The rails are being laid. The institutions are arriving. And for the first time in history, the tools once reserved for the elite are now in your pocket, 24/7.

Do not wait for permission.

*Learn. Adapt. Prosper.*

**Welcome to The New Financial World!**

# Definitions & Terms

## Foundational Concepts

**Blockchain:** A decentralized digital ledger that records data (such as transactions) in a secure, tamper-resistant, and transparent way. It forms the backbone of most cryptocurrencies.

**Cryptography:** The core technology behind cryptocurrencies, ensuring security, privacy, and trust in decentralized digital transactions. It enables secure peer-to-peer exchanges without the need for intermediaries, making cryptocurrencies both reliable and tamper-resistant.

**Cryptocurrency:** A digital form of money that uses cryptography for security and operates on a blockchain. Examples include Bitcoin and Ethereum.

**Decentralization:** A system where control and decision-making are distributed across a network rather than held by one authority.

**Distributed Ledger Technology (DLT):** A decentralized system that uses blockchain technology to record and maintain a secure and transparent record of transactions in a network across multiple participants or nodes.

**Protocol:** Basic sets of rules that allow data to be shared between computers. Cryptocurrencies establish the structure of the blockchain.

**Scalability Trilemma:** A fundamental challenge in blockchain design, stating that it is difficult to achieve high levels of decentralization, security, and scalability simultaneously without trade-offs. Solutions like Layer 2 protocols aim to address this.

**Private Blockchain:** A permissioned blockchain network where access is restricted to a specific group of participants. Unlike public blockchains, only approved users can view data, validate transactions, or operate nodes, making it more controlled, faster, and often used by businesses or organizations.

## Assets

**Crypto Coin:** A cryptocurrency that operates on its own blockchain (ex, Bitcoin, Ethereum).

**Token:** A digital asset built on top of an existing blockchain, such as Ethereum or Solana. Unlike coins, which are native to a blockchain, tokens represent assets, rights, or utilities and rely on smart contracts for functionality. They can represent anything from governance power in a DAO to ownership of a real-world asset, such as real estate, in-app utilities, or artwork. Tokens are widely used in DeFi, gaming, and NFTs.

**Stablecoin**: A cryptocurrency designed to maintain a stable value by pegging to a real-world asset like the U.S. dollar (USD), euro, or even gold.

Top Stablecoins:

- USDT (Tether USDT) USD, fiat-backed (Tether Limited)
- USDC (USD Coin) USD, fiat-backed (Circle)
- DAI USD, over-collateralized crypto (MakerDAO)
- FDUSD (First Digital USD) USD, fiat-backed
- PYUSD (PayPal USD) USD, fiat-backed (issued by Paxos)

- USDP (Pax Dollar) USD, fiat-backed (Paxos)
- GUSD (Gemini Dollar) USD, fiat-backed (Gemini)
- EURC (Euro Coin) EUR, fiat-backed (Circle)
- RLUSD (Ripple USD) USD, fiat-backed (Ripple)

**Non-Fungible Token (NFT):** A unique digital asset representing ownership of a specific item or piece of content. NFTs are distinct and cannot be exchanged on a one-to-one basis.

**Central Bank Digital Currency (CBDC):** Government-issued digital currencies. Unlike stablecoins, they are centralized and regulated. Some examples include: China's Digital Yuan, European pilots, and FedNow-linked discussions. Risks include: surveillance, privacy, and centralization.

**Altcoin:** Any coin that is not Bitcoin.

Top Alt Coins:

- Ethereum (ETH)
- Binance Coin (BNB)
- Solana (SOL)
- Ripple (XRP)
- Bitcoin Cash (BCH)
- Cardano (ADA)
- Arbitrum (ARB)
- Wrapped Bitcoin (WBTC)
- Toncoin (TON)

- Sui (SUI)
- Tron (TRX)
- Polkadot (DOT)
- Bitcoin Cash (BCH)
- Litecoin (LTC)
- Avalanche (AVAX)
- Crypto.com (CRO)
- Stellar (XLM)
- Hedera (HBAR)
- UNUS SED LEO (LEO)
- Filecoin (FIL)
- Aptos (APT)

**Meme coins**: Community-driven crypto tokens inspired by internet culture, fun first, finance second. They are born from internet memes and pop culture and thrive on community, humor, and virality rather than traditional fundamentals. Utility (if any) tends to be experimental or added over time. Prices can move fast and unpredictably, driven by sentiment and social buzz. Treat them as entertainment/collectibles, not as investments.

Top Meme coins:

- Dogecoin (DOGE) Dogecoin chain
- Shiba Inu (SHIB) Ethereum

- Pepe (PEPE) Ethereum
- Floki (FLOKI) Ethereum/BSC
- Baby Doge Coin (BABYDOGE) BSC
- Bonk (BONK) Solana
- dogwifhat (WIF) Solana
- Book of Meme (BOME) Solana
- Popcat (POPCAT) Solana
- Catwifhat (MEW) Solana
- Brett (BRETT) Base
- Jeo Boden (BODEN) Solana
- Myro (MYRO) Solana
- FartCoin (FRTC) Solana
- Wojak (WOJAK) Ethereum
- SPX900 coin (SPX) Ethereum
- ArbDoge AI (AIDOGE) Arbitrum
- Mog Coin (MOG) Ethereum
- Akita Inu (AKITA) Ethereum
- Useless coin (USELESS) Solana
- Husky (HUSKY) Avalanche

- Puggy Penguins (PENGU) Ethereum

- Pitbull (PIT) BSC

**Privacy Coin:** A cryptocurrency designed to enhance user privacy and anonymity in transactions, often using advanced cryptographic techniques like zero-knowledge proofs or ring signatures. Ex. Monero (XMR), Zcash (ZEC).

- **Monero (XMR)** – Strong default privacy using ring signatures and stealth addresses.

- **Zcash (ZEC)** – Optional privacy via zero-knowledge proofs (shielded transactions).

- **Dash (DASH)** – Optional privacy through transaction mixing (PrivateSend).

- **Horizen (ZEN)** – Privacy features combined with a broader blockchain ecosystem.

- **Secret (SCRT)** – Focuses on private smart contracts and encrypted data.

- **Oasis Network (ROSE)** – Enables confidential data processing alongside DeFi.

- **Firo (FIRO)** – Uses advanced cryptography (Lelantus protocol) to enhance anonymity.

- **Grin (GRIN)** – Another Mimblewimble-based coin focused on simplicity and privacy.

- **Verge (XVG)** – Uses network-level privacy (Tor and I2P) to obscure user identity.

**Real-World Assets (RWAs):** Tokenized representations of physical or traditional assets on the blockchain, such as real estate, bonds, or commodities, enabling fractional ownership and instant liquidity. RWAs bridge traditional finance and crypto, with growing adoption in DeFi (e.g., tokenized U.S. Treasuries via platforms like BlackRock's BUIDL).

**Oracle**: A service that provides external, real-world data to smart contracts on the blockchain, enabling them to interact with off-chain information. Risks include data manipulation or failures. Ex: Chainlink (LINK).

**Fork:** A change in the blockchain protocol that creates a new version of the chain.

- Hard forks are not backward compatible (e.g., Bitcoin Cash from Bitcoin)

- Soft forks are backward compatible. Ex. A Word document created in Word 2025 can still open in Word 2010, as long as it does not use new features that the old version cannot understand.

- Backward compatible: Refers to whether new rules or changes can still work with the old version of the software (or blockchain nodes) without breaking anything.

**Wrapped (**coins/tokens): A wrapped token (or wrapped coin) is a tokenized representation of another crypto asset that lives on a different blockchain or in a different token format, while staying pegged 1:1 to the original ("underlying") asset.

**mBridge (Multiple CBDC Bridge):**
A cross-border payment platform developed by central banks to enable faster, cheaper international transactions using central bank digital currencies (CBDCs). It allows participating countries to settle payments directly with each other on a shared blockchain-like infrastructure,

reducing reliance on intermediaries like correspondent banks or systems such as SWIFT.

**Key Participants:**

- Bank for International Settlements (BIS)
- People's Bank of China
- Hong Kong Monetary Authority
- Bank of Thailand
- Central Bank of the United Arab Emirates

**Directed Acyclic Graph**

**(DAG):** A data structure made of nodes connected by directed edges with no cycles (you cannot loop back to the start). In simpler terms, it's like a flowchart where each step leads to the next, but there are no loops or backtracking. A technical/data-structure concept (how information or transactions are arranged).

Some crypto networks use a DAG ledger under the hood and may be governed by a DAO on top. Ex. HBAR, IOTA, NANO

Key traits:

- **Directed:** Each edge has a one-way direction.
- **Acyclic:** No circular paths, so the graph flows in one direction without loops.
- **Partial order:** You can topologically sort nodes, so dependencies come first.

## Consensus Mechanisms

**Hashgraph:** Hashgraph is a new type of technology for recording and sharing data, similar to blockchain, but faster and more efficient. Rather than linking blocks like Bitcoin or Ethereum, Hashgraph uses a faster, more efficient way for everyone on the network to agree on events and their timing. (Ex: HBAR)

Imagine people spreading news in a small town:

1. One person tells two people.
2. Those two tell two more each.
3. The news spreads fast.

That is how Hashgraph spreads information through a process called "gossip about gossip", where computers share both new information and who they heard it from. This helps everyone build a clear picture of what is happening on the network. This technology is special because it has:

- High throughput - Can handle lots of transactions per second
- Low latency - Transactions are confirmed very quickly
- Strong security - Even if some participants try to cheat, the system still reaches the correct result

**Proof of Work (PoW):** A decentralized consensus mechanism that requires members of a network to expend effort solving an arbitrary mathematical puzzle to prevent anybody from cheating the system. It is used by Bitcoin for validating transactions and mining new tokens. (BTC)

**Proof of Stake (PoS):** A consensus mechanism used by Ethereum that significantly reduces the need for computational power. It achieves this by using randomly selected validators to confirm transactions and create new blocks, thereby lowering energy consumption compared to PoW.

**Delegated Proof of Stake (DPoS):** In some blockchain systems (like EOS or Tron), instead of everyone directly validating transactions, the stakeholders (people who hold tokens) vote to choose a smaller group of trusted participants called delegates or "block producers". These delegates are the ones who actually validate transactions and add new blocks to the blockchain.

This setup aims to:

- Increase efficiency since fewer people are doing the heavy work, and transactions are faster.

- Maintain decentralization because the community still decides who the delegates are through voting, so power isn't entirely centralized.

**Proof of History (PoH):** A consensus mechanism used by Solana to establish a historical record by using cryptographic timestamps to ensure the order of transactions, creating a reliable and tamper-proof sequence of events directly within the blockchain.

**Proof of Authority (PoA):** An alternative consensus mechanism that relies on known and reputable validators to produce blocks and provide computational power to a network. Proof of Authority means trusted people, not random users, validate transactions. It is fast and reliable, but less decentralized. (Vechain)

**Proof of Liquidity (PoL):** A type of blockchain that works like Ethereum and runs on its own network (Layer 1). Instead of validators just locking up tokens like in Proof of Stake, they earn rewards by providing liquidity, meaning they put their tokens into trading pools that help the network run smoothly. This connects network security with economic activity, rewarding people who help the system stay active and valuable. It is a value-driven approach that encourages both security and growth.

**Mysticeti**: A fast and efficient system that helps the SUI blockchain agree on transactions. It does not use traditional methods like PoW or PoS

Instead, it is built with a BFT (Byzantine Fault Tolerant (BFT) design that allows many transactions to be processed at the same time. Because it is made for SUI's special object-based system, it can handle lots of activity quickly, making it ideal for decentralized apps (dApps) that need speed and reliability.

## Sustainability & Green Crypto

Proof-of-Stake chains (ETH, ADA) reduce energy consumption. Green mining initiatives include flare gas-powered BTC mining and renewable-powered facilities. ESG crypto projects are gaining traction with investors.

## Security and Technology

**Smart Contract:** A self-executing digital agreement that automatically enforces and executes the terms of a contract based on pre-defined conditions, operating on a blockchain network. They operate on a simple if/then logic.

**Private Key:** A secure code that allows access to your crypto assets (ex, a password).

**Public Key:** A cryptographic code shared publicly, used to receive funds. (Ex: wallet address)

**Know Your Customers (KYCs):** An essential standard in investment and financial services, crucial for verifying customers' identities and economic profiles.

**Seed Phrase (Mnemonic):**

- The human-readable backup for a crypto wallet.
- Typically, consists of 12 words (128-bit entropy + 4-bit checksum) or 24 words (256-bit entropy + 8-bit checksum).

- From this single phrase, all your private keys and addresses can be re-derived. Lose it = lose funds. Share it = give away funds.

**DO NOT:**

- Share your seed phrase with anyone or type it into a website, bot, Google form, "support" chat, or browser extension that asks for it.

- Screenshot it, store it in cloud notes or email, or keep it in plaintext on a computer/phone.

**Bridges:** A crypto bridge is a protocol or mechanism that connects different blockchain networks, enabling the transfer of digital assets, tokens, and data between them, thereby fostering interoperability.

**ZK-proofs:** A zero-knowledge proof (ZKP) is a cryptographic method where one party (the prover) can prove the truth of a statement to another party (the verifier) without revealing any information beyond the fact that the statement itself is accurate. In crypto, ZKPs enhance privacy and scalability by verifying transactions or complex computations without disclosing underlying data.

**Slashing**: In cryptocurrency, slashing refers to a Proof-of-Stake (PoS) protocol mechanism that penalizes validators for violating specific network rules by seizing a portion, or all, of their staked digital assets (tokens). This harsh financial punishment serves to deter malicious behavior or gross negligence, such as double-signing blocks or prolonged downtime, thereby protecting the network's integrity and security.

## Investments & Trading

**Wallet:** A tool (hardware, software, or app) that stores public/private keys to access crypto.

**Hot Wallet:** A type of cryptocurrency wallet that is connected to the internet, making it convenient for accessing and managing your crypto, but also more vulnerable to hacking than cold wallets.

**Cold Wallet:** A cryptocurrency wallet that stays offline, making it much safer from hacking, phishing, and malware. It is ideal for long-term storage of crypto assets, especially in large amounts.

**Exchange:** A platform that allows users to trade cryptocurrencies like Bitcoin (BTC), Ethereum (ETH), and other digital assets.

**Decentralized Finance (DeFi):** A system where control is distributed rather than being centralized by one authority.

**Decentralized Exchange (DEX):** A peer-to-peer (P2P) trading platform without an intermediary (ex, Uniswap, SushiSwap).

**Decentralized Physical Infrastructure Networks (DePIN)**: Blockchain-based systems that use crypto tokens to incentivize individuals and businesses to build, maintain, and expand real-world physical infrastructure. DePINs leverage decentralized networks to make services like data storage, computing power, and wireless networks more accessible, resilient, and affordable than traditional centralized models, creating a self-sustaining ecosystem through a "flywheel" of participant contribution and token rewards.

**Slippage:** This typically occurs because the price of a volatile asset like a cryptocurrency can change rapidly in the brief time between when a trader places an order and when the exchange or blockchain completes the transaction. That is why, typically, your buy price can be higher on centralized exchanges. On a decentralized wallet, you can adjust the slippage percentage.

## DeFi & Financial

**Liquidity Pool:** A collection of cryptocurrencies that facilitate trading, lending, or other DeFi activities without needing a traditional order book or middleman.

**Staking:** A process that allows token holders to earn rewards for helping to secure a proof-of-stake (PoS) blockchain network.

**Yield Farming:** Depositing crypto assets in a liquidity pool DeFi platform to earn higher returns.

**Impermanent Loss:** A temporary decrease in the dollar value of assets a user deposits into a decentralized finance (DeFi) liquidity pool, compared to simply holding those assets in their personal wallet. It occurs because the automated market maker (AMM) rebalances the pool's assets based on their relative prices, leading to the user holding a different ratio of tokens than they started with. The loss is "impermanent" because if the tokens return to their original price ratio, the loss disappears.

**Restaking**: A process that allows stakers to redeploy their already-staked cryptocurrency to secure multiple blockchain protocols simultaneously, earning additional rewards for their participation in different networks. Unlike traditional staking, where staked assets are locked to only one network, restaking extends the trust and security from a primary blockchain (like Ethereum) to other decentralized applications (dApps), such as data availability layers or oracle networks. This creates a marketplace for decentralized trust, enabling new protocols to access a robust security framework more cost-effectively than building their own from scratch, while allowing stakers to amplify their returns.

**Airdrops:** A distribution of free cryptocurrency tokens or NFTs to users' digital wallets, typically serving as a marketing strategy for new blockchain projects to create awareness, attract users, and reward early adopters and community members. Users qualify for an airdrop by meeting certain criteria, such as holding a specific cryptocurrency, using a platform before a certain date, or completing specific tasks, with the goal of distributing tokens and boosting project engagement.

## Standards & Compliance & Future Laws (Neutral Overview)

**ISO 20022:** A global standard that provides a common platform for creating financial messages. It uses:

- A **modeling method** that describes how financial businesses and transactions work, without being tied to any specific programming language or format.

- A **central dictionary** of financial terms and data items, so that everyone in the industry uses the same language and definitions when sending information.

**ISO 27001:** An international standard that certifies an organization has a strong, company-wide information security management system, meaning it follows best practices to protect data, manage risks, and keep information secure.

**SOC 1:** A compliance report that focuses on how a company's internal controls affect its customers' financial reporting, ensuring that financial data handled by the service provider is accurate, secure, and reliable.

**SOC 2**: A report that shows your service follows strict standards for security, availability, processing integrity, confidentiality, and privacy, proving you protect customer data and maintain reliable systems.

**KYC/AML Basics:** Certain services are required by law to verify the identity of their users (Know Your Customer) and monitor transactions for suspicious activity (Anti-Money Laundering) to prevent fraud, money laundering, and other illegal activities.

**CSA STAR (Cloud Security Alliance):** A certification that confirms a company's cloud systems are secure and compliant, ensuring safe and reliable cloud infrastructure for real-world asset (RWA) issuance and trading.

**PCI DSS:** A payment security standard that protects cardholder data during transactions. It is essential for RWA platforms that handle fiat-to-crypto payments or settlements through credit or debit card systems.

## Token Standards

**Satoshi (Bitcoin):** The smallest unit of Bitcoin, used to measure value and enable microtransactions. One Bitcoin (BTC) equals 100 million satoshis, making it possible to divide and transfer very small amounts of value.

**Gwei (Ethereum):** A small unit of Ethereum used to measure transaction fees, known as "gas." One Ether (ETH) equals 1 billion gwei, allowing the network to price computation and transactions in precise, fractional amounts.

**ERC-20:** Ensures that all fungible tokens are identical and work the same way, so they're easy to trade, store, and integrate in DeFi apps.

**ERC-721:** Defines a standard for unique tokens, where each token has its own ID and properties, unlike ERC-20s, which are identical and interchangeable.

**ERC-1155 / ERC-3643:** Support multiple or specialized token types for different use cases.

**ERC-1400 / ERC-3643** (Tokenized Securities Standards): Ethereum standards for security tokens that include features like permissions, KYC, and investor rights, often used in real-world assets (RWA) token frameworks.

**CBDC Anti-Surveillance State Act (often shortened to a "CBDC Act" H.R.5403):** A proposed U.S. House bill that amends the Federal Reserve Act to prohibit certain actions.

- Prevents the Federal Reserve from issuing a retail CBDC or providing services/accounts directly or indirectly to individuals.
- Prohibits the Fed from testing or implementing a retail CBDC without explicit authorization from Congress.
- Passed by the House: July 2025
- Senate Status: Pending

**Financial Innovation & Technology for the 21st Century Act (FIT21 H.R.4763):** A proposed U.S. House bill focused on updating market regulations.

- Clarifies how oversight is split between SEC/CFTC.
- Gives the CFTC spot authority over "digital commodities" in spot markets when certain decentralized criteria are met.
- Creates a framework under which token can be treated as a digital commodity rather than a security if they meet certain criteria (Ex: decentralization)
- Passed by the House: May 22, 2024
- Senate Status: Pending

**Digital Asset Market Clarity Act (Clarity Act of 2025 – H.R.3633):** A proposed law that:

- Defines the criteria in which a digital asset may avoid registration as a security if certain conditions are met. (Ex:Assets on a sufficiently decentralized and mature blockchain)

- Clarifies the oversight responsibilities between SEC/CFTC.
- Passed by the House: July 2025
- Senate Status: Pending

**Guiding and Establishing National Innovation for U.S. Stablecoins Act (The GENIUS Act S.1582):** A landmark U.S. law creating the first comprehensive federal rules for payment stablecoins, digital assets designed to maintain a stable value, typically pegged to a national currency like the U.S. dollar. Key points:

- Requires stablecoin issuers to hold 100% reserves of high-quality assets. (1:1 backing)
- Gives stablecoin holders priority in bankruptcy proceedings.
- Implements strict consumer protection, including anti-money laundering rules.
- Allows approved entities, banks and supervised nonbanks, to issue stablecoins.
- Lays groundwork for international cooperation on stablecoin regulation.
- Enacted into Law: July 2025

**What each does and how they interlock:**

| Bill | Role in the Stack | What it Changes |
|---|---|---|
| FIT21 (Financial Innovation and Technology for the 21st Century Act) | Market Structure & Lanes | Defines when a token/network is a digital commodity (CFTC oversight) vs. a security (SEC oversight); establishes venue rules, disclosures, and regulatory divisions between SEC and CFTC. |
| CLARITY Act (Digital Asset Market Clarity Act, formerly referred to as Securities Clarity Act) | Definition Fix | Clarifies that a token sold via an investment contract isn't itself a security by default; provides pathways for tokens to transition to commodities upon decentralization. |
| GENIUS Act (Guiding and Establishing National Innovation for U.S. Stablecoins Act) | Payment Rails | Creates a federal framework for fiat-backed stablecoins, requiring 1:1 reserves with high-quality assets, redemption rights, bankruptcy priority for holders, AML/consumer protections, and issuer eligibility for banks/nonbanks |
| CBDC Anti-Surveillance State Act | Guardrail | Prohibits the Federal Reserve from issuing a retail CBDC without explicit congressional authorization; restricts any potential CBDC to protect privacy and prevent surveillance. |

**Regulation by Region**

- **U.S.:** The SEC and CFTC remain active regulators.
- **Europe:** Markets in Crypto-Assets Regulation (MiCA) sets a comprehensive crypto framework.·
- **Asia:** Singapore, Hong Kong, and Japan are now developing crypto-friendly regulations and positioning themselves as crypto hubs.

**Web 3 & Finternet**

**Web 3:** The next generation of the internet that is decentralized, user-owned, and blockchain-based.

**Web3 Evolution: Updating the Infographic**

Building on the 2023 infographic, Web3 in 2025 combines Web1's decentralization with Web2's functionality, accruing value to participants. Updates include AI integration and Layer-3 for advanced apps.

| Era | Timeline | Key Features | Governance | Functionality | Who Captures Value |
|---|---|---|---|---|---|
| Web1 | 1990s+ | Open protocols (e.g., email, SMTP, HTTP) | Community | Limited | None to network |
| Web2 | 2005+ | Centralized services (e.g., Google, Meta) | Corporation | Advanced | Big Tech companies |
| Web3 | 2020+ | Blockchain networks (e.g., Bitcoin, Ethereum, L2s/L3s) | Community/ DAOs | Advanced (AI-integrated, scalable) | Network participants (tokens, NFTs) |

This evolution emphasizes user sovereignty, with 2025 trends like DACs and tokenization enhancing portability and privacy.

**Decentralized Autonomous Organization (DAO):** A group or an organization that operates without a central authority, governed by a community based on rules enforced through smart contracts on a blockchain.

**Decentralized Applications (dApps):** Applications that run on a blockchain or peer-to-peer (P2P) network of computers instead of on a single computer. Rather than operating under the control of a single authority, dApps are spread across the network to be collectively controlled by their users.

**Gas Fees:** Charges imposed by blockchain networks to validate transactions.

**Internet of Things (IoT):** A Network of physical objects, sensors, devices, vehicles, or machines used to collect and share data.

- Core: Devices and firmware, connectivity (Wi-Fi, 5G, LPWAN), edge or cloud processing, device management.
- Value: Real-time monitoring and automation.
- Examples: Smart meters, factory robots, connected cars, and wearables.

**Internet of Value (IoV):** The ability to move and settle value (money, assets, rights) across the internet as easily as sending an email.

- Core: Payment rails and ledgers (blockchains, real-time payment systems), digital tokens/stablecoins, wallets, smart contracts.

- Value: Near-instant, programmable, cross-border payments.
- Examples: Sending money with stablecoins, on-chain stocks, micropayments, CBDC pilots.

**Internet of Trust (often "trust layer"):** Standards and systems that make sure people, devices, and data online are authentic and verified. It helps to reduce fraud and ensure that the data is real.

- Core: Public-key cryptography, identity/auth (Digital IDs, verifiable credentials), certificates/attestations, transparency logs, hardware roots of trust.
- Value: Authenticated interactions without relying on a single gatekeeper; reduced fraud and spoofing.
- Examples: Passkeys, device verification, supply-chain tracking, content authenticity (e.g., signed media).

**How they fit together**

- IoT generates data and triggers actions.
- Internet of Trust confirms the data is real and comes from a verified source.
- Internet of Value allows money or assets to move automatically based on that trusted data

Example: A verified sensor detects damage from a verified reading which triggers an automatic insurance payout.

**Finternet (Financial Internet)**: A financial network that moves and manages money digitally. It connects banks, blockchains, payment systems, and market infrastructures so value can move easily and safely across them, just like how information moves across the web. Key traits:

- Interoperability: Different systems (CBDCs, banks, stablecoins, securities) talk to each other via common messaging and settlement standards.

- Programmability: Smart rules/logic (smart contracts, purpose-bound money) allow things like conditional payments or instant trade settlements.

- Built-in Trust & Compliance: Identity, credentials, and policy (KYC/AML, permissions) embedded into the system.

- Data portability: People can safely share financial data between providers with consent.

- Governance: Shared rules and legal frameworks across countries.

**How is it different**

- **Finternet vs. Internet of Value:** IoV is the broad vision of moving value like data; Finternet is a real-world, regulated version that makes it work safely.

- **Finternet vs. Fintech:** Fintech are the apps we use; Finternet is the interoperable infrastructure that connects them.

**Public layer-1 blockchains**

These are the main base networks that other apps and tokens are built on.

- Bitcoin (BTC): Peer-to-peer digital money; strongest focus on security and immutability.

- Ethereum (ETH): General-purpose smart contracts; home to most DeFi/NFT activity.

- Solana (SOL): Designed for speed and low fees; supports fast, high-volume apps.

- XRP Ledger (XRPL): Payments-focused ledger with built-in DEX.
- Cardano (ADA): Research-based blockchain focused on security and sustainability.
- Polkadot: Connects multiple blockchains ("parachains") sharing security.
- Cosmos ("ATOM" ecosystem): Let's independent blockchains ("app-chains") connect and share data via IBC.
- Avalanche: Offers fast finality and supports customizable networks ("subnets").
- Tezos: Emphasizes on-chain governance (self-updating) and secure smart contracts.

**Layer-2 Networks / Ethereum Scaling Solutions**

These work on top of Ethereum to make transactions cheaper and faster.

- Arbitrum, Optimism, Base: Optimistic rollups that process transactions off-chain and settle them on ETH for cheaper and faster transactions.
- zkSync Era, Starknet, Polygon zkEVM: Zero-knowledge (ZK) rollups that improve privacy and scalability.
- Polygon PoS: A popular sidechain that works with ETH for faster, low-cost transactions (often grouped as L2).

**Enterprise / Permissioned Blockchains**

Used mainly by businesses and governments for private or industry-specific networks.

- Hyperledger Fabric: Modular system for private networks; used in supply chain and finance.

- R3 Corda: Designed for financial institutions, supports private, point-to-point workflows (e.g., trade finance).
- Quorum / ConsenSys Quorum: An enterprise version of Ethereum for private use by banks and companies.
- Hyperledger Besu: A business-ready Ethereum client that can run either public or private networks.
- Hedera Hashgraph: A public, council-governed DLT (not a blockchain) built for speed and fairness. Real-World Applications (Built on These Platforms)
- DeFi: Apps like Uniswap and Aave (Ethereum/L2s) for trading and lending.
- Stablecoins: Digital dollars like USDC and USDT issued across Ethereum, Solana, Polygon, and more.
- Supply Chain Tracking: IBM Food Trust (on Hyperledger Fabric) and VeChain for product traceability.
- Trade Finance: Contour networks on Corda for digitizing letters of credit.
- Banking Infrastructure: JPM Coin (on Quorum) used for tokenized deposits and instant settlement.
- Digital Identity: Sovrin / Hyperledger Indy for verifiable credentials and identity verification.
- CBDC/multi-CBDC pilots: Projects like BIS mBridge and similar projects exploring cross-border settlement on DLT.

## Future of Work & Careers in Web3

### Emerging roles

As blockchain and Web3 expand, new jobs are appearing across technology, finance, and governance:

- Blockchain Developers: Build decentralized applications (dApps) and smart contracts.

- Competent Contract Auditors: Review code for vulnerabilities and security flaws.

- DAO Managers: Coordinate operations, proposals, and governance in decentralized organizations.

- Token Economists: Design token systems and incentives that keep decentralized networks sustainable.

- Compliance Officers: Ensure Web3 projects follow laws on finance, privacy, and digital assets.

Certifications from organizations like Blockchain Council or Ethereum Foundation are becoming popular entry points into these careers. Big picture: Entire career paths from finance and development to marketing and law are shifting toward decentralized ecosystems.

## Core Narratives in Crypto & Web3

### Adoption & Macro Trends

- Institutional Adoption & ETFs: Spot BTC (and soon ETH) ETFs normalize crypto in mainstream investment portfolios.

- Stablecoins as "Internet Money": Used for remittances, e-commerce, and cross-border payments like a digital dollar that moves globally.

- Bitcoin as Digital Gold: Its limited supply creates long-term value through predictable "halving" cycles.

- Emerging Markets Use Cases: Helps people hedge against inflation and move money across borders using mobile wallets.

- NFT Art and Collectables: Digital ownership for art, gaming assets, and collectibles (like digital Pokémon cards).

**Infrastructure Evolution**

- Ethereum Scaling (L2s): Rollups (like Arbitrum, Optimism) make apps faster and cheaper, with more integration layers emerging.

- Modular Blockchains: Separate the roles of execution, settlement, and data storage (e.g., Celestia/EigenDA).

- Interoperability: Cross-chain bridges and standards (like Inter-Blockchain Communication Protocol or IBC) make it easier to move assets and liquidity safely between blockchains.

- Bitcoin Layer 2s & Ordinals: Bring programmability and token creation to the Bitcoin network.

- DePIN (Decentralized Physical Infrastructure): Token-powered networks for real-world infrastructure like compute power, sensors, or Wi-Fi.

- AI × Crypto: Combining AI with blockchain to create marketplaces for data, computing power, and verified AI agents.

**Security, Identity, Trust**

- Restaking & Shared Security: Using the same validators, Actively Validated Service(s) (AVSs), to secure multiple blockchain services.

- MEV Minimization & Intents: Protects users from losing value through more intelligent routing.

- Account abstraction & gas sponsorships for mainstream experience.

- Privacy with Zero-Knowledge (ZK) Proofs: Allows selective sharing of information, keeping transactions private but compliant.

**Assets & Finance**

- Real-World Asset (RWA) Tokenization: Bringing traditional assets like treasury bonds, funds, and deposits on-chain.

- DeFi 2.0: Advanced decentralized finance, which includes derivatives, structured products, and improved risk management tools.

- CBDCs & the Finternet: Central bank digital currencies connected through interoperable financial networks for instant, regulated value exchange.

**Consumer & Culture**

- Gaming & NFTs (Utility-First): Game assets, tickets, or loyalty items that can travel across platforms.

- SocialFi & Creator Economy: On-chain social networks where creators and fans share revenue and ownership through tokens.

- Meme Coins: Highly speculative tokens, but powerful for community engagement, marketing, and cultural momentum.

## Ethical & Risk Management (*Read This*)

**Irreversibility:** Once a blockchain transaction is confirmed, it cannot be undone. Always test and verify before sending funds: Double-check wallet addresses and network details.

**Smart-contract risk:** Even smart contracts that have passed audits can contain bugs or vulnerabilities. Never invest or lock up more than you can afford to lose. Use reputable protocols and stay alert to updates or exploits.

**Stablecoin and bridge risk:** Stablecoins rely on different systems to maintain their dollar peg, and bridges carry trust risks when transferring tokens across blockchains. Research how each stablecoin works (e.g., collateralized vs. algorithmic) and only use verified cross-chain bridges.

**Privacy & data hygiene:** Blockchain data is public and traceable. Use best practices:

Avoid reusing the same wallet address repeatedly.

- Don't share wallet addresses tied to your identity.
- Use privacy features or mixers only where legal and compliant.

**Common Scams & Best Practices:** Scams are widespread in crypto. Protect yourself by:

- Diversifying investments.
- Securing private keys offline (hardware or cold wallets).
- Double-checking smart contract links and official sources.
- Ignoring suspicious DMs, links, and "airdrops."

Common scams include:

- Rug pulls: Developers disappear after taking funds.

- Ponzi schemes: Fake yields or guaranteed profits.
- Phishing: Fake websites or wallets steal your keys.
- Fake airdrops: Scams tricking users into signing malicious transactions.

Education and awareness remain the best defense.

**Volatility:** Cryptocurrency prices can fluctuate dramatically due to market sentiment, news, or macroeconomic factors. As of October 2025, the total market cap is around $3.8 trillion, but even major coins like Bitcoin can drop 10% in a single day. Stay diversified and avoid emotional trading.

**Regulatory Risks:** Rules differ worldwide and can change quickly. Key areas:

- **U.S.:** SEC enforcement actions affecting tokens and exchanges.
- **EU:** MiCA (Markets in Crypto-Assets) framework providing more precise regulation.
- **Other regions:** Some countries still restrict or ban crypto.

Always report taxes (e.g., capital gains) and comply with local laws.

**Security Risks:** Hacks, scams, and exchange failures remain significant threats. Examples include the FTX collapse (2022) and numerous DeFi exploits.

Best practices:

- Use hardware wallets for long-term storage.
- Verify official URLs and social accounts.
- Avoid keeping large balances on exchanges.

**Environmental Impact:** Energy consumption from PoW mining contributes to carbon emissions. Transitioning to Proof-of-Stake (PoS) systems helps reduce energy usage and environmental impact.

**Adoption Barriers:** Mainstream adoption is slowed by:

- Technical complexity.
- Scalability issues.
- Interoperability challenges between networks.

Progress continues through:

- Tokenized assets
- Institutional adoption (e.g., ETFs surpassing $10B+ in inflows by 2025).

**Market Trends (August 2025):** Institutional adoption accelerating with ETF inflows; altcoin rallies in DeFi and AI-driven projects; short-term corrections amid rate cuts and geopolitical uncertainty; focus on sustainable, long-term growth over hype.

## Taxes

### Capital Gains Tax

- **Short-Term Gains**: If you held crypto 1 year or less, it is taxed as ordinary income (10-37% based on income bracket).
- **Long-Term Gains**: If you held crypto more than 1 year, it is taxed at a lower rate between 0-20% based on income.
- **Calculation**: Gain = Sale price - Cost Basis (original purchase price + transaction fees). Losses can offset gains. Ex: Buy 1 BTC at $30,000, sell at $50,000. Gain = $20,000, taxed based on holding period.

### Income Tax

- Crypto received from mining, staking, airdrops, or crypto payments for services or work is taxed as ordinary income at fair market value (FMV) when received.
- Example: Earn 0.1 ETH staking when ETH = $2,000. Report $200 as income.

### Record-Keeping

- Track every transaction: Date and time, amount, FMV in USD, fees, and purpose (e.g., purchase, sale, trade).
- Use crypto tax software (e.g., CoinTracker, Koinly) to sync data from exchanges and wallets automatically.
- Keep records for at least 3-7 years for potential IRS audits.

### Reporting

- **Form 8949 & Schedule D**: Report capital gains and losses from crypto sales or trades.
- **Schedule 1 or C**: Report crypto income (e.g., staking, mining, or payments) as "other income" or business income if self-employed. Use Schedule C if it is part of a self-employed business.
- **Form 1099**: Exchanges like Coinbase may issue 1099-MISC or 1099-B for certain transactions, but not all activity is reported to the IRS. It is still your responsibility to track.

### Tips

- **Loss Harvesting**: Sell crypto at a loss to offset gains, reducing your tax bill.
- **Donations**: Donating crypto to an approved charity can avoid

capital gains tax and may be deductible.

- **FIFO vs. Specific ID**: IRS usually assumes you sell your oldest coins first (First-In-First-Out or FIFO). However, you can use Specific Identification to choose which coins to sell for tax optimization. Just make sure to keep detailed records.
- **DeFi & NFTs**: These are taxable, too. Trading NFTs or earning rewards from DeFi platforms can create capital gains or income taxes.

# Historical Events

**The Fall of Mt. Gox. The Day Bitcoin Shook the World (2014)**

In Bitcoin's early days, Mt. Gox was not just an exchange; it was the exchange. At its peak, it handled over 70% of the world's Bitcoin trades, acting as the gateway for thousands of early adopters. For many, it was the symbol of the crypto revolution.

But in February 2014, that dream collapsed. Hackers breached Mt. Gox's systems, stealing a staggering 850,000 BTC. At the time, the loss was valued at roughly $450 million. Today, it would be worth tens of billions.

The incident sent shockwaves through the crypto world. Investors panicked. Trust was shattered. Regulators, who had been watching the space cautiously, suddenly saw proof that the digital gold rush came with real risks. Lawsuits mounted, executives resigned, and the company fell into bankruptcy.

Yet, from this disaster came one of crypto's most important lessons: security must come first. Mt. Gox's downfall marked the birth of stricter industry standards and inspired the creation of stronger, more resilient exchanges that still stand today.

**OneCoin The Billion-Dollar Illusion (2014–2017)**

Imagine a charismatic leader, a "visionary" promising a cryptocurrency that would dethrone Bitcoin and change global finance forever. That was the story sold by Ruja Ignatova, the self-styled “Cryptoqueen,” who launched OneCoin in 2014.

Her pitch was irresistible: a global payment network, lightning-fast transactions, and guaranteed wealth for early adopters. Investors poured in money, billions of dollars from more than 175 countries. Motivational seminars, flashy presentations, and luxury events gave the illusion of legitimacy.

But behind the shine, there was no blockchain. No innovation. No cryptocurrency at all. OneCoin was a Ponzi scheme, designed to funnel billions into the pockets of its creators.

By 2017, as authorities closed in, Ruja vanished without a trace. She became one of the FBI’s Most Wanted fugitives, her empire collapsing overnight, leaving investors with over $4 billion in losses and millions of defrauded investors.

The OneCoin saga became a global cautionary tale. In a world driven by hype and innovation, trust must be verified, not assumed. It pushed regulators toward greater transparency and investor protection across the blockchain industry.

**The FTX Collapse When the King Fell (2022)**

During the 2021 bull run, FTX emerged as one of the fastest-growing crypto exchanges in history. Its founder, Sam Bankman-Fried (SBF), was hailed as a prodigy, the “JP Morgan of crypto.” FTX’s slick branding, sports sponsorships, and celebrity endorsements made it the darling of Wall Street and Silicon Valley alike.

Then, in November 2022, the empire unraveled. Investigations revealed that FTX had secretly funneled billions of dollars of customer funds into its sister company, Alameda Research, to cover trading losses and make risky bets.

When the truth surfaced, confidence vanished overnight. Within days, FTX went from a $32 billion powerhouse to bankruptcy. More than

$8 billion in customer funds disappeared, leaving millions of users stranded. SBF was arrested and charged with fraud, money laundering, and conspiracy. His trial became one of the most closely watched financial scandals of the decade, reshaping the crypto landscape forever.

FTX's downfall served as a turning point for regulators worldwide. Governments accelerated crypto oversight, exchanges tightened security protocols, and investors learned a painful but lasting lesson. Trust must be earned even in a decentralized world.

Representing the most defining moments in crypto's short but turbulent history. They exposed the risks of greed, poor security, and lack of transparency, while shaping the safer, more mature ecosystem we see today.

The crypto world has survived scandal after scandal, emerging stronger each time. But one lesson echoes louder than ever. In this new financial frontier, trust is everything.

And as the ecosystem evolves fast, with the rise of energy-efficient blockchains, sustainable innovations, and borderless finance, the next generation of financial systems is not coming; it is already here.

# Resources


Berwick, A. (2025, September 1). *Trump Family Amasses $5 Billion Fortune After Crypto Launch*. Retrieved from The Wall Street Journal: https://www.wsj.com/finance/currencies/trump-family-amasses-6-billion-fortune-after-crypto-launch

Binance Research (Moulik Nagesh, Joshua Wong, Michael JJ, Asher Lin Jiayong). (2025, July 17). *Half-Year Report 2025*. Retrieved from Binance: www.binance.com/en/research/analysis/half-year-report-2025

bitbo.io. (2025). *microstrategy*. Retrieved from bitbo.io: https://bitbo.io/treasuries/microstrategy

Burnett, S. (2025, July 18). *Decentralized Finance DeFi) Market Statistics 2025: TVL, Token Caps & User Adoption Revealed*. Retrieved from CoinLaw: https://coinlaw.io/decentralized-finance-market-statistics/

**Cryptoslav, I. (2022). *The OneCoin Scam: the Dazzling Story of the Biggest Crypto Ponzi in History*. Retrieved from coinmarketcap: https://coinmarketcap.com/academy/article/the-onecoin-scam-the-dazzling-story-of-the-biggest-crypto-ponzi-in-history**

**Edition, C. (2025, February 19). *altcoin-season-mia-raoul-pal-reveals-crypto-portfolio-puts-sui-ahead-of-solana*. Retrieved from coinedition.com: https://coinedition.com/altcoin-season-mia-raoul-pal-reveals-crypto-portfolio-puts-sui-ahead-of-solana/**

**Hassan, A. (2025, August 26). *tom-lee-calls-eth-bottom*. Retrieved from Yahoo Finance: https://finance.yahoo.com/news/tom-lee-calls-eth-bottom-083124320.html**

**Hitchcock, L. (2025, September 1). *The 10 Public Companies With the Biggest Bitcoin Portfolios*. Retrieved from Yahoo Finance: https://finance.yahoo.com/news/10-public-companies-biggest-bitcoin-193206248.html**

**https://solanacompass.com/learn/Superteam/macro-investing-hedge-funds-and-crypto-ft-real-vision-founder-raoul-pal-superteam-podcast**

**Hwan Kim, A. D.-T. (2025, March 27). *Consumer Finance and Fintech Blog*. Retrieved from Sheppard Mullin: https://www.consumerfinanceandfintechblog.com/2025/03/from-seizures-to-strategy-the-u-s-governments-move-toward-a-national-crypto-reserve/**

***ISO 20022*. (n.d.). Retrieved from ISO 20022: https://www.iso20022.org**

**Kaur, G. (2024, June 26). *The Mt. Gox Bitcoin heist, and why it still matters*. Retrieved from cointelegraph: https://cointelegraph.com/learn/articles/the-mt-gox-bitcoin-heist**

**MarketMinute. (2025, September 9). *DeFi's Dual Horizon: Innovation Soars Amidst Persistent Challenges*. Retrieved from Financial Content: https://markets.financialcontent.com/stocks/article/marketminute-2025-9-9-defis-dual-horizon-innovation-soars-amidst-persistent-challenges**

**https://youtu.be/IEmTkDCIuz8?si=KGpMcrvrPoeEqV4i - youtube.com/@PaulBarronNetwork- crypto crash 0ct102025**

**Insider trading, engineered liquidation suspicions grow as crypto market crashes - Cryptopolitan https://share.google/sOotrctpwN10T4aSQ**

**Reiff, N. (2024, October 10. *What Went Wrong with FTX*. Retrieved from Investopedia: https://www.investopedia.com/what-went-wrong-with-ftx-6828447**

**Shapshak, T. (2018, November 27). *How Mobile Money Continues to Boom in Africa*. Retrieved from Forbes: https://www.forbes.com/sites/tobyshapshak/2018/11/27/how-mobile-money-continues-to-boom-in-africa/**

**Shin, E. (2025, August 26). *cathie-wood-net-worth*. Retrieved from datawallet: https://www.datawallet.com/crypto/cathie-wood-net-worth**

**Shipra. (2025). *Decoding DeFi Trends Every Investor Should Know in 2025*. Retrieved from SoluLab: https://www.solulab.com/decoding-defi-trends/**

**Spong, R. (2025, January). *ITFA's Fintech Committee's Top Priorities for 2025*. Retrieved from International Trade and Forfaiting Association (ITFA): http://www.itfa.org**

***The Economist: Get Ready for a World Currency*. (2021, March 28). Retrieved from Internet Archive: https://archive.org/details/the-economist-get-ready-for-a-world-currency**

**Ethereum Foundation – Transaction finality**
**https://ethereum.org/en/developers/docs/consensus-mechanisms**

**Bitcoin.org – Irreversible transactions**
**htps://bitcoin.org/en/you-need-to-know**

**Official documentation**
**https://nexusmutual.io**

**Chainanalysis – Crypto Crime Reports**
**https://www.chainalysis.com/reports**

**Ronin Network ($625M, 2022)**
**https://blog.chainalysis.com/reports/ronin-bridge-hack-2022**

**Poly Network ($611M, 2021)**
**https://www.coindesk.com/tech/2021/08/10/poly-network-hack-explained**

**Wormhole ($325M, 2022)**
**https://www.coindesk.com/tech/2022/02/02/wormhole-bridge-hack-explained**

**Nexus Mutual whitepaper**
**https://docs.nexusmutual.io**

**Fidelity Digital Assets – Crypto vs traditional assets reports**
**https://www.fidelitydigitalassets.com/research**

**Delphi Digital – DeFi insurance deep dives**
**https://members.delphidigital.io**

**CoinDesk – Why DeFi insurance isn't a silver bullet**
**https://www.coindesk.com/learn**

**Raoul Pal, Real Vision – Global liquidity & crypto cycles**
**https://www.realvision.com**

**Bank for International Settlements (BIS) –**
**Global liquidity & risk appetite**
**https://www.bis.org**

**Vatalik: An Ethereum Story - is a feature-length documentary released in late 2024 that chronicles the life of Vitalik Buterin and the evolution of the Ethereum network.**

**<u>Other Notable Sources:</u>**

**Coinpedia.com**

**defillama.com**

**twitter.com**

**Coinmarketcap.com**

**consumerfinanceandfintechblog.com**

**Ccn.com**

**Coingecko.com**

**Finance.yahoo.com**

**twitter.com/DPGmaximus/YouTube**

**www.youtube.com/@Parker_Ray**

**www.youtube.com/@blackrue**

**www.youtube.com/@ApexCryptoConsultingNFA**

**www.youtube.com/@NoBsCryptoOfficial**

**www.youtube/@JakeGordonCrypto**

**www.youtube.com/@PaulBarronNetwork**

# About the Author

Zakir Sadiki is a blockchain, cryptocurrency educator and independent financial systems researcher with a background in asset management and electrical reliability. His work with large-scale infrastructure that must perform under stress and uncertainty shaped his understanding of resilience, not just in machines, but in financial systems. He began trading traditional stocks a year before the COVID-19 market crash, witnessing firsthand how liquidity shocks and policy decisions ripple through global markets. That experience sparked his ongoing research into blockchain, decentralized finance, and the future of money. The New Financial World distills those insights for everyday readers who want to understand how finance is evolving clearly, practically, and without hype.

www.ingramcontent.com/pod-product-compliance
Lightning Source LLC
LaVergne TN
LVHW022059200926
848481LV00003B/992
*9798950412028*